Dysteleology

Dysteleology

A Philosophical Assessment of
Suboptimal Design in Biology

Michael Berhow

☙PICKWICK *Publications* · Eugene, Oregon

DYSTELEOLOGY
A Philosophical Assessment of Suboptimal Design in Biology

Copyright © 2019 Michael Berhow. All rights reserved. Except for brief quotations in critical publications or reviews, no part of this book may be reproduced in any manner without prior written permission from the publisher. Write: Permissions, Wipf and Stock Publishers, 199 W. 8th Ave., Suite 3, Eugene, OR 97401.

Pickwick Publications
An Imprint of Wipf and Stock Publishers
199 W. 8th Ave., Suite 3
Eugene, OR 97401

www.wipfandstock.com

PAPERBACK ISBN: 978-1-5326-6158-7
HARDCOVER ISBN: 978-1-5326-6159-4
EBOOK ISBN: 978-1-5326-6160-0

Cataloguing-in-Publication data:

Names: Berhow, Michael, author.

Title: Dysteleology : a philosophical assessment of suboptimal design in biology / by Michael Berhow.

Description: Eugene, OR: Pickwick Publications, 2019 | Includes bibliographical references.

Identifiers: ISBN 978-1-5326-6158-7 (paperback) | ISBN 978-1-5326-6159-4 (hardcover) | ISBN 978-1-5326-6160-0 (ebook)

Subjects: LCSH: Intelligent design (Teleology) | Religion and science | Naturalism | Natural theology | Science—Philosophy

Classification: BL240.2 B27 2019 (print) | BL240.2 (ebook)

Manufactured in the U.S.A.   06/07/19

To Becky,
for being my wonderful wife and best friend
and to Gus, Frankie, and Alasdair
for making our home lively
and always entertaining

Contents

Preface | ix
Acknowledgements | xv

1. Suboptimal Design in Biology | 1
2. A Scientific Critique of Design in Biology | 21
3. A Theological Critique of Design in Biology | 54
4. Defending Intelligent Design Scientifically | 71
5. Defending Intelligent Design Philosophically | 94
6. Making Darwin a Gift to Science and Religion | 119

Bibliography | 141

Preface

SINCE MY FRESHMEN YEAR of college, I have been fascinated with questions that blur the lines between science, religion, and philosophy. How did life begin? What is unique about being human? Is evolution compatible with belief in God? Can science provide evidence for God's existence? Where did our sense of wonder come from? Why is there something rather than nothing? What is beauty? Questions like these regularly captured my imagination as a young eighteen-year-old, though I had no idea that various answers to these questions could generate controversy.

As a sophomore, while taking a course in human anatomy, I got my first taste of such a controversy. Our professor was an engaging and charismatic lecturer, who, throughout the semester, frequently ridiculed an idea called intelligent design (ID). I had never heard of ID, so I never quite understood what or whom he was critiquing. During one of his lectures, while covering the intricate structure of the eye, he took time to demonstrate that the physiology of sight is inconsistent with the notion of an intelligent designer. He diagramed on the whiteboard the path that light must travel to make vision possible—stating that light must enter the cornea, pass through the pupil to the back of the eye, eventually hitting the retina, which contains millions of photoreceptors—the cones and rods that convert light into electrical signals. When light hits the retina, however, our professor explained that it must first travel through a series of ganglion and bipolar cells before reaching the cones and rods. The light then produces chemical changes within those cones and rods, which becomes the electrical signal that flows back through the bipolar and ganglion cells to the optic nerve. After seeing this path diagramed, it seems counterintuitive from an engineering perspective, and so our professor sarcastically exclaimed, "Some intelligent design!"

This particular moment made a profound impression on me, mainly because I remember how passionate our professor was while delivering his lecture. He almost seemed upset, like he was arguing with someone. Later in the semester, it became clear that he was arguing with Christians who believe in a particular doctrine of creation. Before one of his lectures, he opened class with a lengthy announcement, stating that he would appreciate it if students would stop sending him Christian hate mail. I thought his announcement was strange, since I never made the connection that his criticisms of ID might be construed as an attack against Christianity. Apparently other students, however, saw the connection clearly.

When class ended, I walked back to my dorm room to search online for resources related to Christianity and ID. I found several websites, with some seemingly more credible than others. As I read through various articles online, I began to learn about various conflicts pertaining to Christianity and science. I learned that some Christians advocate for young earth creationism, whereas others support old earth creationism. I learned about a small group of Christian biologists and apologists who critiqued evolution and argued for creationism. As I kept reading, my excitement for learning more about this issue grew substantially.

After several hours of internet research, I felt pretty informed on the debate between creationism and evolution. So I sent an email to my professor later that evening—hoping to clear up some issues for him. Here is part of what I wrote (sent April 1, 2004):

> Dear Professor,
>
> It has been interesting being in your anatomy class this last semester. You are one of the best professors I have ever had. Today in class you mentioned how people have been emailing you saying that you should not pick on God or the Bible. I hope this letter does not come across that way. I know that no matter what I say you will believe what you believe because you have the information to back up what you believe. I also hope you know that no matter what you say I will believe what I believe because I have the information to back up what I believe. Every comment you have made in class against Christianity has an objection. There are intelligent Christian biologists who have scientific theories on creationism. Maybe their views are not right; however, they have just as much proof as the theories on evolution. I do not take any

offense to what you say in class because it has not changed my view on Christianity or evolution.

Again I want to say I respect you as a professor, and as a person. I do not hold any grudges against you. My purpose of this letter is to address some mindless Christian hate letters you may have received. I hope and pray you will not take this the wrong way. If you want to reply, you may.

Also, I have heard you talk much about your evolution class in lecture. I will not be able to take it during the summer, but I would like some information over what you teach. I am a sucker for knowledge, especially when dealing with this topic.

Thank you very much for reading this letter, and for any information you could send me.

Sincerely,

Michael Berhow

As I reflect on this email fifteen years later, I can think of many things I wish I had said differently. What I could not have anticipated, however, was that sending this email would become a life-changing experience for me. My professor did respond, and his response both frustrated me and sparked a deep desire to learn everything I could about creationism, evolution, and ID. For the next few years, we corresponded back-and-forth through email, and our correspondences ultimately led me to connect with other classmates to start a creation/evolution student group on campus.

My newfound passion also motivated me to drop my pre-physical therapy major, and instead I began to take classes in philosophy and religion. For example, I took a course in philosophy where we covered the basic arguments for God's existence. That was when I realized that ID is seemingly connected to a particular version of the teleological argument—expressed most clearly in William Paley's watchmaker argument. My anatomy professor was familiar with this connection, and he once reminded me that Charles Darwin's *Origin of Species* was published after Paley's *Natural Theology*—suggesting that biology no longer needs teleology. I soon started to realize that we live in a post-Paley world, which helped me understand why ID might be scorned within the scientific community.

Outside the academy, however, I noticed that Paley's legacy endures. Early in college, a friend handed me *Unlocking the Mystery of Life*—a documentary produced by the Discovery Institute—a public policy think tank in Seattle, WA. This documentary introduced me to some of the major ID theorists, such as Michael Behe, Michael Denton, Phillip Johnson, Paul Nelson, Jonathan Wells, Stephen Meyer, and Dean Kenyon. Johnson's name especially stuck out to me, since he had recently delivered a lecture at my university. I immediately bought and read his book *Darwin on Trial*, which introduced me to the worldview dimensions of the debate over evolution. Specifically, Johnson argued that ID, properly understood, is the worldview alternative to Darwinism. He described Darwinism, moreover, as a perspective on evolution that rules out intelligent causation before examining the relevant evidence. As such, Johnson maintained that Darwinism is a form of religion.

During my senior year of college, I took a break from studying ID and turned my attention to the so-called New Atheists, mainly because I wanted to make sure I was being intellectually honest with my faith. I first read *The God Delusion* by Richard Dawkins. At that time, Dawkins brought up arguments against God's existence that I had never considered. And while he never persuaded me to become an atheist, he did cause me to reevaluate some of my beliefs—including my beliefs about ID. The argument that stuck out to me most was the problem of suboptimal design in biology, since that was the argument my anatomy professor had frequently articulated in class. Put simply, the argument states that if the world of biology is filled with numerous dysfunctions, then God could not be responsible for designing life. If he were, then he would also be responsible for suboptimal design. But God, by definition, is not a suboptimal designer. My solution to this problem was simple—I affirmed the existence of God while rejecting the notion of ID.

After college, my interest in the relationship between science and Christianity continued to grow. This led me into seminary where I discovered the works of Francisco Ayala. Ayala's books were a breath of fresh air, since he expressed some of the conclusions I had about God and the nature of design in biology. While working on my PhD, I decided to focus my research on Ayala's solution to natural evil in biology, articulated most clearly in *Darwin's Gift to Science and Religion*. To do this effectively, my advisor recommended that I compare Ayala's work with William Dembski's for my dissertation project. He further challenged me to track down and read everything written by both authors before developing a conclusion. While I cannot say that I read *everything* written by Ayala and Dembski, I do think I have read all of their works related to ID, evolution, teleology, Darwin, natural evil, and suboptimal design. As a result, my understanding and appreciation of the debate over ID has been greatly enriched.

I also came to conclusions that I did not anticipate. Before beginning my project, I was unimpressed with ID. My original goal was to build upon Ayala's insights regarding natural evil, and then use those arguments to address the specific problem of suboptimal design in biology. Engaging with Dembski's work was simply an academic exercise intended to demonstrate that I was a careful and balanced scholar. I did not expect that Dembski would change my mind and attitude on several issues related to ID, and I especially did not expect that my central argument against ID—namely, the existence of suboptimal design in biology—would be relatively easy to explain from an ID perspective. This book is thus an attempt to explain why I changed my mind about the problem of suboptimal design in biology, and why I no longer see it as a problem for ID.

Acknowledgements

THERE ARE MANY PEOPLE who helped make this book possible. I am particularly thankful to those who have encouraged and coached me through my research. Ted Cabal (my PhD advisor) mentored me as a young seminary student, stimulated my passion for philosophy, and then motivated me to pursue a PhD after seminary. More than anyone else, Cabal pushed me to pursue scholarly excellence by providing numerous critiques and suggestions on each chapter of this work. James Parker, likewise, was significant for my academic development. He befriended me in seminary, and his courses taught me how to think about my scholarship from a distinctly Christian perspective.

Outside of my academic mentors from seminary, I am thankful to Douglas Blount, Mike Hildreth, Dennis Helder and Greg Peterson for reading and offering valuable comments on early drafts of this manuscript. I am also thankful to James Tour for encouraging me to continue exploring the topic of intelligent design, and for connecting me with The Discovery Institute's CSC Seminar on Intelligent Design in the Natural Sciences. That experience both challenged and enhanced my understanding of intelligent design, so I am grateful to both Tour and The Discovery Institute for making that opportunity available.

In addition to all those who inspired me academically, I am thankful for my wife, Becky, for working countless hours as a nurse, supporting us through seminary, and being an amazing mother to Gus, Frankie, and Alasdair. I could not have accomplished any of this without my wonderful and supportive family. God is faithful!

1

Suboptimal Design in Biology

A COMMON THEOLOGICAL CRITIQUE of intelligent design (ID) centers on the problem of dysteleology. This problem states that because there are clear examples of suboptimal design in biology, life is probably not the product of an engineer-like designer. If it were, then one could argue that the designer is less than fully competent. ID critic Francisco Ayala expresses this critique in the following question: "If functional design manifests an Intelligent Designer, why should not deficiencies indicate that the Designer is less than omniscient, or less than omnipotent?"[1] This book provides a philosophical analysis of two approaches to answering this question, one offered by Ayala and the other offered by William Dembski, a leading ID theorist.

In *Darwin's Gift to Science and Religion*, Ayala describes numerous examples of defects and dysfunctions in the natural world—arguing that such examples undermine ID and support Darwinian evolution. Ayala further claims that Darwinian evolution is a friend, rather than a foe, to religion. To make this claim, he contends that Darwin's theory provides insight into the nature of biology that allows theologians to rethink the role of design in living systems. Darwin, according to Ayala, removed teleology from biology. This is good news for religion because it presumably gets God off the hook for a specific type of natural evil, namely, the existence of suboptimal structures and systems in biology.

Ayala's claim is theological in nature, but my goal is to evaluate his claim philosophically to determine whether the problem of suboptimal design in biology undermines the general notion of ID. My evaluation,

---

1. Ayala, *Darwin's Gift*, 22.

in other words, focuses more on the *nature of Nature* than it does on the *nature of the Divine*. Given that there are examples of suboptimal design in biology, I want to determine whether a dysteleological perspective on biology is more plausible than a teleological perspective. To determine this, we need not engross ourselves in theological issues, since one can affirm the existence of teleology in biology without affirming the existence of God.[2] My central thesis, therefore, is that while Ayala may provide useful *theological insights* into the problem of dysteleology, he fails to show how his argument undermines the central notion ID—that "there are telltale features of living systems and the universe that are best explained by an intelligent cause . . . rather than an undirected material process."[3] Put simply, I argue that suboptimal design in biology does not support Ayala's nonteleological conception of nature.

Background

Dysteleology is a philosophical concept that describes the non-existence of τέλος (*telos:* meaning end, purpose, or goal) or design in nature. The term itself originated from Ernst Haeckel's *The History of Creation* (1884), where he explains,

> The infinite importance of the study of rudimentary organs for the fundamental questions of natural philosophy cannot be too highly estimated; we might set up with their aid a theory of the *unsuitability of parts* in organisms, as a counter-hypothesis to the old popular doctrine of the *suitability of parts*. This latter dualistic teleology finally leads us to supernatural dogmas and miracles, whereas we obtain from the former, monistic dysteleology, a firm foundation for our mechanical interpretation of nature.[4]

---

2. As I mention elsewhere, there are several historical and current examples of nontheistic philosophers and scientists who argue for a teleological outlook on nature. Plato, Aristotle, and Cicero, for example, all argued for the existence of design in nature. To provide some current examples, Michael Denton, an early pioneer of ID, considers himself an agnostic. See Denton, *Evolution*. And Thomas Nagel, though he does not identify as an ID proponent, is an atheist who argues for a teleological conception of nature. See Nagel, *Mind & Cosmos*. Likewise, Bradley Monton is an atheist philosopher who publically defends ID. See Monton, *Seeking God in Science*. One can safely conclude, therefore, that belief is God is not a prerequisite for becoming an ID advocate.

3. Meyer, *Signature in the Cell*, 4.

4. Haeckel, *History of Creation*, 1:331.

Haeckel's argument is that nature is not consistent regarding the suitability of parts within organisms. Some organisms display features of intricate optimality, but others do not. If one interprets optimal design as evidence for teleology, then Haeckel maintains that one should interpret examples of suboptimal design as evidence for dysteleology. To argue otherwise would lead to a dualistic interpretation of nature, which presumably undermines the practice of science.

Many atheists, Haeckel included, expanded the notion of dysteleology into an argument against the existence of God. Proponents of such *dysteleological arguments* do not attempt to disprove God's existence, but rather they endeavor to provide support for a moderate version of atheism.[5] Their argument might be stated as a narrative, wherein Charles Darwin delivered the last blow to the design argument for God's existence, thus undermining a central argument for theism.

According to this narrative, William Paley (1802) was working with the best knowledge available to him when constructing his famous teleological argument.[6] Paley maintained that there "cannot be design without a designer; contrivance without a contriver; order without choice," and then skillfully presented numerous cases of apparent design in nature.[7] As science progressed in the nineteenth century, however, Darwin introduced an alternative explanation for the contrivances of nature. He proposed that natural selection acting upon variations within organisms could sufficiently explain the apparent design of life.[8] For many, this proposal

---

5. By moderate atheism, I am referring to what Antony Flew called "the presumption of atheism" (Flew, "Presumption of Atheism," 19–32). This perspective is sometimes called *negative atheism*, *weak atheism*, or *soft atheism*. In short, moderate atheists attempt to clarify the meaning of atheism by proposing that atheism is not a positive position. It does not assert the non-existence of God, rather it "lacks belief" when it comes to any theistic or supernatural claim. On this view, atheism is considered a default position. When a theist argues for the existence of God, therefore, he bears the full burden of proof. If an atheist successfully undermines the theist's arguments, then atheism is considered more reasonable by default.

6. Agreeing with this sentiment, Ayala writes, "Paley elaborated the argument-from-design with greater cogency and more extensive knowledge of biological detail than had any other author, before or since" (Ayala, "From Paley to Darwin," 58).

7. Paley, *Natural Theology*, 12.

8. Darwin's specific contribution (along with Alfred Russel Wallace) to evolutionary theory was the idea of natural selection. There were many before Darwin who argued that organisms go through variations and change over time. Georges Cuvier, James Hutton, Jean-Baptiste Lamarck, Robert Edmond Grant, Étienne Geoffroy Saint-Hilaire, Erasmus Darwin, and Robert Jameson all demonstrated this idea. Darwin argued that natural

represents a watershed moment in the field of biology, because Darwin offered a plausible naturalistic mechanism to explain biological diversity *without divine intervention*.[9]

In addition to this achievement, Darwin's theory also solved problems that Paley's thesis seemingly produced—most notably the problem of suboptimal design.[10] Richard Dawkins explains the problem as follows:

---

selection operates on variations, causing some organisms to flourish and others to suffer extinction. He wrote, "Let it be borne in mind how infinitely complex and closefitting are the mutual relations of all organic beings to each other and to their physical conditions of life. Can it, then, be thought improbable, seeing that variations useful to man have undoubtedly occurred, that other variations useful in some way to each being in the great and complex battle of life, should sometimes occur in the course of thousands of generations? If such do occur, can we doubt (remembering that many more individuals are born than can possibly survive) that individuals having any advantage, however slight, over others, would have the best chance of surviving and of procreating their kind? On the other hand, we may feel sure that any variation in the least degree injurious would be rigidly destroyed. This preservation of favourable variations and the rejection of injurious variations, I call Natural Selection" (Darwin, *Origin of Species*, 63).

9. Concerning whether a designing agent was involved in the process of evolution, Darwin writes, "If we must compare the eye to an optical instrument, we ought in imagination to take a thick layer of transparent tissue, with a nerve sensitive to light beneath, and then suppose every part of this layer to be continually changing slowly in density, so as to separate into layers of different densities and thicknesses, placed at different distances from each other, and with the surfaces of each layer slowly changing in form. Further we must suppose that there is a power always intently watching each slight accidental alteration in the transparent layers; and carefully selecting each alteration which, under varied circumstances, may in any way, or in any degree, tend to produce a more distinct image. We must suppose each new state of the instrument to be multiplied by the million; and each to be preserved till a better be produced, and then the old ones to be destroyed. In living bodies, variation will cause the slight alterations, generation will multiply them almost infinitely, and natural selection will pick out with unerring skill each improvement. Let this process go on for millions on millions of years; and during each year on millions of individuals of many kinds; and may we not believe that a living optical instrument might thus be formed as superior to one of glass, as the works of the Creator are to those of man?" (Darwin, *Origin of Species*, 141–42). In this passage, Darwin implicitly agues that God is not needed for biological development, at least not in the way Paley suggested. For Darwin, natural selection working upon variations over millions of years is sufficient to explain the design of complex organisms like the eye.

10. Paley did address the problem of suboptimal design in *Natural Theology*, and I will explicate his response in chapter 2. In short, Paley argued that examples of suboptimal design do not negate positive evidences for design (see Paley, *Natural Theology*, 37). Of course, one could also appeal to certain ideas derived from traditional Christian theology, such as the doctrine of the fall, to overcome the problem of suboptimal design.

SUBOPTIMAL DESIGN IN BIOLOGY

> Darwinism raises our consciousness [regarding suboptimal design]. Evolved organs, elegant and efficient as they are often are, also demonstrate revealing flaws—exactly as you'd expect if they have an evolutionary history, and exactly as you would not expect if they were designed. I have discussed examples in other books: the recurrent laryngeal nerve, for one, which betrays its evolutionary history in a massive and wasteful detour on its way to its destination. Many of our human ailments, from lower back pain to hernias, prolapsed uteruses and our susceptibility to sinus infections, result directly from the fact that we now walk upright with a body that was shaped over hundreds of millions of years to walk on all fours. Our consciousness is also raised by the cruelty and wastefulness of natural selection. Predators seem beautifully 'designed' to catch prey animals, while the prey animals seem equally beautifully 'designed' to escape them. Whose side is God on?[11]

Dawkins's comments and rhetorical question resembles Haeckel's dysteleological argument. If optimal design provides support for God's existence, then suboptimal design should presumably support atheism. Dawkins thus asserts that Paley's argument now seems unfounded given what we have learned from Darwin.[12]

Dawkins pushes his argument further, claiming that as our understanding of science increases, naturalistic explanations continually replace theistic explanations. Darwin was the most important expressions of this trend, because according to Dawkins, Paley's design argument was the only persuasive argument left for theists. He explains,

> It is sometimes said that [David Hume] disposed of the Argument from Design a century before Darwin. But what Hume did was criticize the logic of using apparent design in nature as *positive* evidence for the existence of God. He did not offer any *alternative* explanation for apparent design, but left the question open. An

---

11. Dawkins, *God Delusion*, 161.

12. In numerous places throughout the *Origin of Species*, Darwin highlights imperfections within the natural world—arguing that these imperfections fit well within a survival-of-the-fittest perspective on nature. He explains, "Natural selection tends only to make each organic being as perfect as, or slightly more perfect than, the other inhabitants of the same country with which it has to struggle for existence. And we see that this is the degree of perfection attained under nature. . . . Natural selection will not produce absolute perfection, nor do we always meet, as far as we can judge, with this high standard under nature. The correction for the aberration of light is said, on high authority, not to be perfect even in that most perfect organ, the eye" (Darwin, *Origin of Species*, 151).

5

atheist before Darwin could have said, following Hume: 'I have no explanation for complex biological design. All I know is that God isn't a good explanation, so we must wait and hope that somebody comes up with a better one.' I can't help feeling that such a position, though logically sound, would have left one feeling pretty unsatisfied, and that although atheism might have been *logically* tenable before Darwin, Darwin made it possible to be an intellectually fulfilled atheist.[13]

Dawkins further suggests that Darwin's great accomplishment was to remove the need for teleological explanations in biology. Natural selection, he writes, "not only explains the whole of life; it also raises our consciousness to the power of science to explain how organized complexity can emerge from simple beginnings without any deliberate guidance."[14] And without deliberate guidance in biology, Dawkins cannot think of any scientific evidence left to demonstrate God's existence.[15] For this reason, he contends that the existence of God is highly improbable for those who care about science.[16]

13. Dawkins, *Blind Watchmaker*, 10.

14. Dawkins, *God Delusion*, 116.

15. Of course, there are still many attempts to provide scientific arguments for the notion of design, as well as for God's existence. The development and continued success of big bang cosmology, for example, has aided many apologists in developing sophisticated versions of the cosmological argument. See Copan and Craig, Kala[set macron over a]m *Cosmological Argument*. There are also fine-tuning arguments that provide compelling reasons to think that our planet and the physical constants of the universe were deliberately adjusted for the purpose of sentient life on earth. See Gonzalez and Richards, *Privileged Planet*; Lewis and Barnes, *Fortunate Universe*. For my purposes, however, I will not explore claims of deliberate guidance outside the area of biology. Within the biological sciences, there seems to be a consensus that naturalistic mechanisms are sufficient for explaining the apparent design of organic life. These explanations rely heavily upon methodological naturalism (MN), a philosophical position that is contested by ID advocates. In my review of Dembski's work, I outline some basic arguments against MN and in favor of actual design within biology. For further ID arguments against MN in biology, see Behe, *Darwin's Black Box*; *Edge of Evolution*; *Darwin Devolves*; Johnson, *Darwin on Trial*; *Reason in the Balance*; Meyer, *Darwin's Doubt*; *Signature in the Cell*; Axe, *Undeniable*.

16. Dawkins, *God Delusion*, 51. Dawkins defines his perspective as *De facto* atheism. He expresses this perspective when he writes, "I don't know for certain but I think God is very improbable, and I live my life on the assumption that he is not there" (Dawkins, *God Delusion*, 51), and then illustrates it by explaining that most people are atheists when it comes to "Zeus, Apollo, Amon Ra, Mithras, Baal, Thor, Wotan, the Golden Calf and the Flying Spaghetti Monster. I just go one god further" (Dawkins, *God Delusion*, 53). While Dawkins is convinced that God is not real, his *De facto* atheism is appropriately classified

I reference this moderate version of atheism, because Ayala's main argument against ID ironically resembles Dawkins's case against theism. The difference is that Ayala turns the dysteleological argument on its head by making it an apologetic *for theism*, minus any teleological conception of nature. He does this by suggesting that ID is poor theology, and therefore does not represent a coherent version of theism. He agrees with Dawkins that Darwin overturned the design argument, and thus demonstrated that God did not create biological life. He disagrees with Dawkins, however, regarding his atheistic conclusions. For Ayala, Darwin is a gift for theists because Darwin's theory reveals that God is not responsible for suboptimal design. This preserves the notion of divine goodness by making natural selection the solution to physical evil. Ayala explains,

> Traditional theology distinguishes three kinds of evil: (1) moral evil or sin, the evil originated by human beings; (2) pain and suffering as experienced by human beings; (3) physical evil, such as floods, tornados, earthquakes, and the imperfections of all creatures. Theology has a ready answer for the first two kinds of evil. Sin is a consequence of free will; the flip side of sin is virtue, also a consequence of free will.... [But] what about earthquakes, storms, floods, droughts, and other physical catastrophes? Enter modern science into the theologian's reasoning. Physical events are built into the structure of the world itself.[17]

Ayala, therefore, agrees with Dawkins when he contends that Darwin's great contribution to modern science was to show that "nothing in the world of nature escapes the scientific mode of knowledge."[18] In other words, nothing in the world of nature is designed.

---

as moderate atheism, since he does not refer to atheism as a positive position. Science and religion scholars often argue that skeptics like Dawkins wrongly use scientific resources when exploring theological issues. These scholars maintain that the disciplines of science and theology, while certainly in dialogue, represent two separate modes of inquiry. Dawkins responds to this type of critique in his response to Stephen Jay Gould's NOMA proposal. He asks, "Why shouldn't we comment on God, as scientists? And why isn't Russell's teapot, or the Flying Spaghetti Monster, equally immune from scientific skepticism? As I shall argue in a moment, a universe with a creative superintendent would be a very different kind of universe from one without. Why is that not a scientific matter?" (Dawkins, *God Delusion*, 55). This response represents a version of scientism, where science is held as the only (or at least the most significant) form of knowledge.

17. Ayala, *Darwin's Gift*, 3–4.
18. Ayala, "From Paley to Darwin," 57.

And herein lies Ayala's theological critique of ID. ID advocates presumably fail to appreciate the theological benefits of affirming a reality where all physical events are "built into the structure of the world itself." Those who argue (like Paley) that God is responsible for beautiful and complex physical events are, according to Ayala, inadvertently ascribing dishonorable attributes to God's character. He debates this point on the basis of consistency. If God is responsible for *some design*, then God apparently must be responsible for *all design*.[19] This implies that God designed eyes with blind spots, human jaws that are too small for teeth, birth canals that are too narrow for easy passage of the infant's head, spontaneous miscarriages, cancer cells, sickle-cell anemia, and all the other dysfunctional and cruel peculiarities of life.[20] Theological speaking, Ayala maintains that the implications of ID support the notion that God is either not omnibenevolent, or omnipotent. He therefore encourages religious believers to reject ID.

To evaluate Ayala's dysteleological critique of ID, I compare his work to Dembski's. I do this because Dembski is one of the leading thinkers in the ID movement. As of 2016, he was a Senior Fellow with the Discovery Institute's Center for Science and Culture, and is currently a Senior Research Scientist with the Evolutionary Informatics Lab.[21] He has published numerous mathematical and philosophical articles related to ID. His educational credentials include master's degrees in statistics, mathematics, philosophy, and divinity (two from the University of Chicago, one from the University of Illinois, and one from Princeton Theological Seminary). He has two Ph.D.s, one in philosophy from the University of Illinois and one in mathematics from the University of Chicago. He has completed postdoctoral work at MIT, Princeton, Northwestern University, the University of Notre Dame, and the University of Chicago. For most of his

---

19. Taken at face value, Ayala's consistency critique of ID does not seem persuasive. Behe, for example, explains why such a complaint is wrongheaded when he writes, "One difficulty of writing a book questioning the sufficiency of Darwin's theory is that some people mistakenly conclude you're rejecting it in toto. It is time to get beyond either or thinking. Random mutation is a completely adequate explanation for some features of life, but not for others. This book looks for the line between the random and the nonrandom that defines the edge of evolution" (Behe, *Edge*, 14). In chapters 2 and 3, I offer additional support to Ayala's consistency critique before rejecting it.

20. Ayala, *Darwin's Gift*, 154–60.

21. Dembski announced his official resignation from the ID community and the Discovery Institute on September 10, 2016. Even so, he did not repudiate any of his works and he is still associated with Robert Marks's Evolutionary Informatics Lab and the Walter Bradley Center for Natural and Artificial Intelligence.

career, his research interests included ID, complexity theory, information, cryptography, chaos theory, and probability theory. More recently, he has focused on the connections between freedom, technology, and education. He has authored or co-authored at least eleven books, edited or co-edited several more, and published numerous articles in academic books and journals. As for his academic posts, Dembski has taught in several seminaries and Christian universities, including Southern Evangelical Seminary, Southwestern Baptist Theological Seminary, The Southern Baptist Theological Seminary, and Baylor University.

Dembski's scientific work on ID can be found in several works, most notably in *The Design Inference: Eliminating Chance Through Small Probabilities*. Dembski describes this work as a scientific analysis of the connections linking chance, probability, and intelligent causation. It explores ideas and methods closely related to probability and complexity theory, and Dembski argues throughout the book that there is an objective criterion to determine whether an event is derived from intelligent causation. Specifically, Dembski calls this criterion specified complexity (SC) or complex specified information (CSI). He argues that when any event X exhibits features that are both specified and complex, one can reasonably infer that X is the result of design. Dembski's method is certainly relevant to the ID debate; however, the implications of his work expand well beyond the limits of the natural sciences. He proposes that *The Design Inference* is also relevant for forensic scientists, SETI researchers, insurance fraud investigators, debunkers of psychic phenomena, intellectual property attorneys, investigators of data falsification, cryptographers, parapsychology researchers, and programmers of (pseudo-) random number generators.[22]

No Free Lunch: Why Specified Complexity Cannot be Purchased without Intelligence was Dembski's second scholarly work, which was the product of a $100,000 research grant issued by the Templeton Foundation. Whereas *The Design Inference* sought to develop an objective method for detecting design, *No Free Lunch* utilized that method to demonstrate that chance mutations and natural selection working together are incapable of generating SC.[23] Dembski's goal in his second book was to reintroduce the idea of *actual* design in biology. He emphasizes the notion of *actual* design, "because design in biology so often connotes apparent design."[24] Dembski's

---

22. Dembski, *Design Inference*, xii.
23. Dembski, *No Free Lunch*, xiii.
24. Dembski, *No Free Lunch*, xvii.

clarification between apparent and actual design is significant, since it elucidates what the word "intelligent" means in *intelligent* design. By describing *intelligent* design as mere *actual* design, Dembski also implies that *intelligent* design is not necessarily *optimal* design. This clarification will be crucial for evaluating Ayala's dysteleological critique of ID.

After Dembski's initial academic publications, he released several other books intended for a general audience. The most notable is *The Design Revolution: Answering the Toughest Questions about Intelligent Design*. This book is significant because it directly and extensively defends the claim that ID is a respectable scientific research program. In the preface, Dembski writes,

> This book is my attempt to cut through the red tape, psychological inertia and mental cobwebs that prevent intelligent design from receiving fair consideration. In short, it is my attempt at some much needed house cleaning. Even so, my hopes for this book would fall short if a clean house were its only outcome. Besides cleaning house, this book aspires to provide a powerful new vision of science and the world, one that people will want to pursue because they find it so attractive.[25]

While one could dispute whether Dembski truly provides "a powerful new vision for science and the world," *The Design Revolution* does provide several helpful clarifications regarding the scientific project of ID. Specifically, it defines the fundamental claim of ID as follows: "there are natural systems that cannot be adequately explained in terms of undirected natural forces and that exhibit features which in any other circumstance we would attribute to intelligence."[26] Building on this definition, Dembski further describes the scientific work of ID as follows:

1. Producing an objective method (SC) that distinguishes *intelligent causation* from *chance* or *necessity*.
2. Producing scientific and/or mathematical arguments that demonstrate the inadequacy of Darwinian mechanisms to produce SC.
3. Producing evidence that supports the claim that there are certain features in the natural world that cannot be explained by undirected natural forces.

---

25. Dembski, *Design Revolution*, 27–28.
26. Dembski, *Design Revolution*, 27.

When I refer to the "science of ID" or "ID as a scientific research project" throughout this book, I will refer to one of these three statements.

Dembski's philosophical and theological works are also significant.[27] The three most noteworthy are *Intelligent Design: The Bridge between Science and Theology*, *The End of Christianity: Finding a Good God in an Evil World*, and *Being as Communion: A Metaphysics of Information*. In *The Bridge between Science and Theology*, Dembski broadens his definition of ID, calling it a "scientific research program that investigates the effects of intelligent causes; an intellectual movement that challenges Darwinism and its naturalistic legacy; and a way of understanding divine action."[28] The additional category in this definition describes ID as *a way of understanding divine action*. This fourth description shows that ID can function as theological research project, and as such should be distinguished from the scientific research project of ID.[29]

It may be helpful to mention that these two distinct research projects have caused confusion among ID critics. Is ID a scientific research program or a theological research program? In his article "Intelligent Design: The Faith That Dare Not Speak Its Name," Jerry Coyne draws attention to the confusion raised by this question. His article begins with an attempt to discredit ID by emphasizing so-called discrepancies within ID literature. He specifically cites two passages by Dembski, one claiming that ID is "not an evangelical Christian thing, or a generally Christian thing or even a generically theistic thing."[30] In the next passage, Dembski writes, "any view of science that leaves Christ out of the picture must be seen as fundamentally deficient."[31] After citing these passages next to each other, Coyne asks,

27. There is a certainly an overlap between Dembski's scientific and theological work, and therefore I am not making strict distinctions. Dembski's scientific work often addresses philosophical issues that some science and religion scholars consider metaphysical or theological in nature. Likewise, his theological work often explores issues that are generally viewed as restricted to scientific investigation. By referring to some of Dembski's works as scientific and others as theological, therefore, I am simply attempting to classify the general themes of each work.

28. Dembski, *Bridge*, 13.

29. In a later chapter, I provide additional details regarding the distinctions between ID as a scientific research program and ID as a theological research program. While many ID advocates insist that ID is not a theological research program, Dembski's ID project is certainly theological, since he defines ID as "a way of understanding divine action."

30. Dembski, *Design Revolution*, 25.

31. Dembski, *Bridge*, 206.

> Well, which is it? Is ID merely a sophisticated form of biblical creationism, as most biologists claim, or is it science—an alternative to Darwinism that deserves discussion in the science classroom? As the two quotations above imply, you won't find the answers in the writings of the leading advocates of ID. The ambiguity is deliberate, for ID is a theory that must appeal to two distinct constituencies. To the secular public, ID proponents present their theory as pure science. This, after all, is their justification for a slick public-relations campaign promoting the teaching of ID in the public schools. But as is clear from the infamous "Wedge Document" of the Discovery Institute, a right-wing think tank in Seattle and the center for ID propaganda, intelligent design is part of a cunning effort to dethrone materialism from society and science and replace it with theism. ID is simply biblical creationism updated and disguised to sneak evangelical Christianity past the First Amendment and open the classroom door to Jesus. The advocates of ID will admit this, but only to their second constituency, the sympathetic audience of evangelical Christians on whose support they rely.[32]

Coyne's conspiracy theory, represented in the paragraph above, characterizes the type of critique usually raised against ID advocates. And yet, this kind of critique displays an obvious ignorance of basic distinctions clarified by ID thinkers. One only needs to read the full paragraph of Dembski's first quote to see this ignorance. Dembski writes,

> This is not a book in which I address the theodicy problem (I plan to address it in a future book on Genesis, theodicy and the Christian doctrine of creation). Although theodicy is, to be sure, the thorniest problem facing theologians trying to make sense of intelligent design, it is not a problem for intelligent design per se. Intelligent design attempts to understand the evidence for intelligence in the natural world. The nature and, in particular, the moral characteristics of that intelligence constitute a separate inquiry. Intelligent design has theological implications, but it is not a theological enterprise. Theology does not own intelligent design. *Intelligent design is not an evangelical thing, or a generically Christian thing or even a generically theistic thing.* Anyone willing to set aside naturalistic prejudices and consider the possibility of evidence for intelligence in the natural world is a friend of intelligent design.[33]

32. Coyne, "Intelligent Design," 3–4.
33. Dembski, *Design Revolution*, 25.

Only by refusing to include the whole paragraph could one think that Dembski is appealing to "two distinct constituencies." Dembski does think ID is a scientific research program, and much of his contribution to ID develops that case. He is also a Christian theologian who thinks ID has theological implications.

Recognizing the distinction between Dembski's scientific and theological interests should be straightforward, especially since such distinctions are common for science and religion scholars. Ayala, for example, makes the same kind of distinction when he explores the theological implications of evolution. He writes,

> I shudder in terror at the thought that some people of faith would implicitly attribute [the calamity of the natural world] to the Creator's faulty design. I rather see it as a consequence of the clumsy ways of the evolutionary process. The God of revelation and faith is a God of love and mercy, and of wisdom. Darwin's theory of evolution is a gift to science, and to religion as well.[34]

This passage shows that Darwinian evolution has theological implications for Ayala, but that does not suggest that Darwinian evolution is unscientific. In fact, Ayala claims that Darwin's theory is a gift both to science *and* to religion—indicating that Ayala, like Dembski, is pursuing two related but distinct research programs. One is a scientific research program related to Darwinian evolution, and the other is a theological research program related to the theological implications of Darwinian evolution. Just as Ayala explores the relationship between Darwinism and theology, so Dembski explores the relationship between ID and theology. The similarities and differences between Ayala and Dembski make these theologians suitable dialogue partners.

Ayala's academic and religious biography is equally impressive. He was ordained as a Dominican priest in 1960, but resigned from the priesthood in the same year. In 1964, he graduated from Columbia University with a Ph.D. in biology, studying under the prominent geneticist and evolutionary biologist Theodosius Dobzhansky. Ayala was a longtime professor of biological sciences, philosophy, and logic at the University of California, Irvine. His research is grounded in evolutionary biology, and includes research on the origin and evolution of introns, as well as the evolution and functional significance of pseudogenes and ectopic expression. He has contributed to research projects focusing on gene organization, gene regulation, and

---

34. Ayala, *Darwin's Gift*, xi.

the origin, function, and evolution of small RNAs, particularly in parasitic protozoa. In addition to his scientific research, Ayala has contributed to scholarship in the philosophy of biology, the relationship between science and religion, and teaching evolution within public schools.

Ayala has published several books devoted to evolutionary theory, notably *Human Evolution: Trails from the Past*, *Am I a Monkey? Six Big Questions about Evolution*, *The Big Questions: Evolution*, and most recently an edited work entitled, *Essential Readings in Evolutionary Biology*. Closely related to the topic of evolution, he has also written two books in the area of science and religion, namely, *Darwin and Intelligent Design* and *Darwin's Gift to Science and Religion*. A common theme throughout all of his works is that evolution is scientifically credible, it does not contradict religious belief, and that intelligent design is incompatible with both science and theology. In the prologue of *Darwin and Intelligent Design*, he writes,

> There are many believers in the United States and elsewhere who think that science, and particularly the theory of evolution, is contrary to the teachings of the Bible and to religious beliefs, such as Creation by God. Science has demonstrated again and again, beyond reasonable doubt, that living organisms evolve and diversify over time, and that their features have come about by natural selection, a process that accounts for their design. . . . It may surprise you, dear reader, but I will argue that evolution is more compatible with Christianity than "intelligent design" and other creationist theories.[35]

Ayala's unique perspectives on the relationship between Christianity, evolution, and ID make him an intriguing dialogue partner for Dembski.

Explanation of the Problem

In *Darwin's Gift to Science and Religion*, Ayala expounds upon his dysteleological argument against ID. He writes,

> I assert that scientific knowledge, the theory of evolution in particular, is consistent with a religious belief in God, whereas Creationism and Intelligent Design are not. This point depends on a particular view of God—shared by many people of faith—as omniscient, omnipotent, and benevolent. This point also depends on our knowledge of the natural world and, particularly,

35. Ayala, *Darwin and Intelligent Design*, vii–ix.

of the living world. The natural world abounds in catastrophes, disasters, imperfections, dysfunctions, suffering, and cruelty. Tsunamis bring destruction and death; volcanic eruptions erased Pompeii and Herculaneum, killing all their citizens; floods and droughts bring ruin to farmers. The human jaw is poorly designed, lions devour their prey, malaria parasites kill millions of humans every year and make 500 million sick. I do not attribute all this misery, cruelty, and destruction to the specific design of the Creator. About 20 percent of all human pregnancies end in spontaneous abortions during the first two months. That is 20 million natural abortions every year. I shudder in terror at the thought that some people of faith would implicitly attribute this calamity to the Creator's faulty design.[36]

For Ayala, the existence of natural evil highlights an inconsistency between theism and ID. Again, he explains,

> People of faith would do well to acknowledge Darwin's revolution and accept natural selection as the process that accounts for the design of organisms, as well as for the dysfunctions, oddities, and cruelties that pervade the world of life. Evolution makes it possible to attribute these mishaps to the natural processes (which have no moral implications) rather than to the direct creation of specific design of the Creator.[37]

The overall argument here is simple, and it presents a direct challenge for theologians espousing ID. If examples of exquisite design highlight the intelligence of God, then examples of careless and cruel design should highlight the incompetence of God. Ayala insists upon theological consistency regarding this issue. To clarify the argument further, I offer the following outline:

1. A God who is omniscient, omnipotent, and benevolent would not create organisms with suboptimal design (assumption).
2. There are organisms that display features of suboptimal design in biology (as suggested by modern science).
3. ID states that functional organisms were created by God (Ayala's definition of ID).

---

36. Ayala, *Darwin's Gift*, xi.
37. Ayala, *Am I a Monkey?*, 78.

4. If functional organisms were created by God, then one should also assume that organisms displaying features of suboptimal design were also created by God (Ayala's assumed implication of 3).
5. ID assumes that God created organisms that display features of suboptimal design (3 and 4).
6. ID is inconsistent with a God who is omniscient, omnipotent, and benevolent (1 and 5).
7. On the other hand, the theory of evolution states that *all organisms* originated through purely natural processes (Ayala's definition of evolution).
8. If all organisms originated through purely natural processes, then organisms that display features of suboptimal design also originated through purely natural processes (the logical implication of 7).
9. To state that organisms originated through purely natural processes implies that God did not create those organisms (clarification of 7 and 8).
10. The theory of evolution states that God did not create organisms that display features of suboptimal design (7, 8, and 9).
11. The theory of evolution is consistent with a God who is omniscient, omnipotent, and benevolent (1 and 10).
12. ∴ An omniscient, omnipotent, and omnibenevolent God is more consistent with evolution than with ID (6 and 11).

According to the argument above, examples of suboptimal design in nature provide defeaters for ID. By suboptimal design, I include any statement from Ayala that illustrates various kinds of natural evil—tsunamis, droughts, floods, etc.—design peculiarities—the backwards neural wiring of photoreceptors in the retina of human eye, the size of the female birth canal in humans, the panda's thumb, etc.—suggested cruelty—predation, animal suffering, etc.—or simply the general wastefulness displayed in the processes of evolution—survival-of-the-fittest.

While this problem is fairly straightforward, I should make two important clarifications. First, this book presents a broad perspective on the problem of suboptimal design, making it look almost indistinguishable from the problem of natural evil. The reason I do not call it the problem of natural evil is because the problem of natural evil is put forward as a defeater for Christian theism. Both Ayala and Dembski, however, agree that natural evil does not successfully undermine Christian theism. This means that the relevant problem is not the problem of natural evil, but the problem of suboptimal design. According to this problem, as articulated in the argument above, suboptimal design provides a defeater for ID and any teleological conception of nature. Ayala agrees with this claim, whereas Dembski rejects it.

My second clarification refers to the scope of my thesis. Ayala argues that Darwin is a gift to theology precisely because Darwin discovered natural selection, an unguided mechanism that gets God off the hook for all examples of suboptimal design. My goal is not to analyze the merits of his evolutionary theodicy, nor is it to propose an alternative theodicy that is consistent with Christian theism. Rather, my goal is twofold. First, and more modestly, I seek to demonstrate that Ayala's theological argument fails to undermine ID and a teleological conception of nature. Second, and more ambitiously, I seek to demonstrate that Ayala's theodicy (or any evolutionary theodicy) requires a teleological conception of nature to avoid the trap of being self-referentially incoherent. Such an argument may seem counterintuitive, but the form of my argument is similar to arguments that seek to demonstrate the self-defeating nature of maintaining that evolution and naturalism/materialism are both true.[38]

Methodology

There are three methodological issues to mention regarding my approach to this project. First, I limit the scope of my research primarily to the works of Dembski and Ayala. This limitation is required because one can find copious amounts of books and articles written on the topic of ID. To survey the entire corpus of ID literature, therefore, would require more time and research than is available for this project.[39] When necessary, however, I do consult the works of other prominent scholars and scientists.

Second, I devote two chapters to explaining the scientific arguments for and against ID. Such attention may initially seem unwarranted, since I am providing a philosophical assessment of Ayala's dysteleological argument against ID. It will become apparent, however, that Ayala's dysteleological

---

38. For two examples, see Plantinga, *Where the Conflict Really Lies*; Nagel, *Mind & Cosmos*.

39. For details regarding the origin, history, and scope of modern ID arguments, see Woodward, *Doubts about Darwin*.

critique of ID is rooted in his scientific understanding of ID and biological evolution. One cannot properly analyze his dysteleological critique, therefore, without first examining his scientific argument for evolution and his scientific critique of ID. Likewise, Dembski's scientific work is also important, since it provides a basis for ascertaining whether Ayala's portrayal of ID accurately corresponds to ID *as articulated by its proponents*. If Ayala inaccurately represents the scientific program of ID, then the force of his dysteleological critique will likely diminish.

The last methodological issue to consider is my process of evaluation. The first section of this book considers Ayala's scientific and theological critiques of ID. My goal in this section is to summarize, highlight, and analyze central points in Ayala's case against ID. In the second section, I articulate relevant aspects of Dembski's ID project to juxtapose his project against Ayala's critique of ID. This is where most of my assessment takes place. After carefully comparing the arguments of Ayala and Dembski, I develop my central thesis in my concluding chapter, arguing that a teleological conception of nature is necessary to make any evolutionary theodicy logically coherent.

Chapter Summaries

Chapter 2 includes a summary and explanation of Ayala's scientific critique of ID. His arguments against ID have five steps. First, he begins by narrating the history of Paley's watchmaker argument to Darwin's theory of evolution. Before *The Origin of Species* (1859), scientists and intellectuals generally believed that God created life. Ayala reports that such beliefs were respectable in the early nineteenth century because Paley's *Natural Theology* (1802) characterized the most promising science among his contemporaries. Darwin, however, provided a new way of seeing the world. His greatest achievement, according to Ayala, was to show how complex organisms could arise through purely natural processes. The following three steps of Ayala's critique outlines the evidence for biological evolution and explains why Darwin's theory has endured over one hundred and fifty years and why reputable scientists no longer question its validity. His last step provides a direct scientific critique of ID.

Chapter 3 summarizes and explains Ayala's theological critique of ID. This critique centers on his dysteleological argument. In short, Ayala argues that if *apparent* design provides adequate evidence for concluding *actual* design, then one should consistently argue that *apparent* suboptimal design provides adequate evidence for concluding *actual* suboptimal design. Such a conclusion, from Ayala's perspective, is problematic theologically because it undermines the goodness and wisdom of God. Ayala argues, therefore, that ID is poor science and poor theology. Darwin, on the other hand, is a gift for the theologian, since Darwin's great accomplishment was to demonstrate how life could arise without divine intervention. This means that God is not responsible for suboptimal design, rather suboptimal design is the result of undirected processes expressed through random mutation and natural selection.

Chapter 4 summarizes and explains Dembski's method for detecting design. The first section covers his fundamental argument in *The Design Inference*, specifically concentrating on his Explanatory Filter, the concept of specified complexity, and his criteria for detecting agency. Section two provides an overview of *No Free Lunch*, which applies Dembski's idea of specified complexity to biology. Throughout this chapter, I compare Dembski's arguments with Ayala's and argue that the fundamental difference between the two centers on one's ability to detect teleology in nature. Ayala argues that the concept of teleology was undermined by Darwin's theory, and design is therefore not detectable. Dembski, on the other hand, argues that teleology is real and detectable in biology.

Chapter 5 summarizes and explains Dembski's metaphysical commitments. I draw upon Dembski's various philosophical and theological writings but give special attention to his most recent book, *Being as Communion*. I highlight that Dembski's main philosophical contribution centers on the idea that prime reality consists of information, rather than unthinking material atoms. Dembski's information-theoretic conception of nature is purely metaphysical, but it underscores a crucial issue for this book. If design cannot be detected in nature because the natural world is reduced to material substances, then it seems to suggest that any examples of teleology (including human inventions) are ultimately reduced to nonteleological matter. Dembski argues that this position is self-defeating, and should be replaced with an information-theoretic perspective on reality.

Chapter 6 concludes with a final analysis of Ayala's theological critique of ID, along with an argument for the necessity of teleology. I first demonstrate that Ayala is unsuccessful in undermining Dembski's articulation of ID. I then propose that teleology is necessary for developing a coherent evolutionary theodicy. This proposal may seem counterintuitive for many advocates of evolutionary theodicy; however, my argument is related to other arguments that seek to demonstrate the inconsistency between naturalism and evolution.

2

A Scientific Critique of Design in Biology

AYALA CLAIMS THERE ARE two fundamental problems with ID. The first problem is that ID lacks scientific cogency, and the second is that it lacks religious merit by ascribing unacceptable characteristics to God.[1] This chapter critically examines and evaluates Ayala's former contention, that ID lacks scientific cogency. He defends this thesis repeatedly throughout various books and articles, and the outline of his argument appears to follow five steps.[2] First, he contends that the design argument was stated most persuasively in Paley's *Natural Theology* in 1802, but that it was later overturned by Darwin in *The Origin of Species* in 1859. Ayala recounts the history of Paley to Darwin in detail, providing charitable explanations of each thinker's arguments. His second step is to demonstrate that modern scientific discoveries have firmly established Darwin's theory. In step three he presents the case for human evolution, and steps four and five provide more direct critiques of ID. Step four, specifically, elucidates how natural selection has the power to create organisms that appear designed for a purpose, while step five seeks to demonstrate how various arguments offered by ID advocates fail to appreciate the explanatory power of Darwin's articulation of natural selection.

---

1. Ayala, *Darwin's Gift*, 135.
2. While I draw on various sources from Ayala in this chapter, the five steps I mention represent differing chapters in his book, *Darwin and Intelligent Design*. I am not sure whether Ayala views each chapter as a building case against ID, or whether he has two projects in mind (one a case for evolution, and one a case against ID). Either way, Ayala certainly presents ID as an idea in conflict with biological evolution, and therefore evidence for evolution is presumably evidence against ID.

My main goal in this chapter is to explain and assess each step of Ayala's scientific critique of ID. To do this, I compare Ayala's arguments against ID with counterarguments offered in Dembski's textbook on ID, *The Design of Life* (coauthored with Jonathan Wells), though I also draw on other ID sources when necessary. After this assessment, I conclude that Ayala's scientific arguments against ID are unpersuasive when compared to the writings of leading ID advocates.

William Paley to Charles Darwin

Ayala begins his evaluation of ID by providing a historical analysis regarding the demise of teleological explanations in science. He focuses specifically on the history leading up to Darwin's famous discovery of natural selection. Before Darwin, Ayala notes that Paley's watchmaker argument was the most respected and sophisticated version of the design argument to date, and furthermore that the modern ID movement is simply a revival of Paley's project.[3] He concedes that the design argument was persuasive in the early 1800's, but further contends that Darwin ultimately refuted Paley's project. Ayala recounts this history because he thinks Paley offers the most compelling design argument to date.[4] If he is correct, then presumably one does not need to examine the literature of modern ID theorists.

To assess whether Ayala is correct in his analysis, I will briefly consider his retelling of the Paley to Darwin story. He begins by highlighting how Paley's monumental work, *Natural Theology*, built upon several earlier works, most notably John Ray's *Wisdom of God Manifested in the Works of the Creation* (1691). Paley's project, in other words, was not created in a vacuum. Instead, Paley enhanced Ray's thesis by providing meticulous

3. Dembski disagrees with Ayala on this point. He writes, "Paley's business was natural theology. Intelligent design's business is much more modest: it seeks to identify signs of intelligence to generate scientific insights. Thus, instead of looking to signs of intelligence to obtain theological mileage, as Paley did, intelligent design treats signs of intelligence as strictly part of science" (Dembski, *Design Revolution*, 64).

4. Ayala, *Darwin and Intelligent Design*, 3. Elsewhere, Ayala writes that Paley's natural theology was a "brilliant exposition of the argument-from-design, the most articulate and biologically expert case made to date for the existence of the Creator, elicited from the complex functional design of organisms" (Ayala, "From Paley to Darwin," 50). Ayala further argues that Paley developed the case for design with "greater cogency and more extensive knowledge of biological detail than had any other author, before or since" (Ayala, "From Paley to Darwin," 58). I will demonstrate in chapter 4 that Ayala misunderstands the nuances between Paley's *Natural Theology* and modern versions of ID.

details regarding the complexities of mammalian eyes, the precise mechanical arrangement of bones, cartilage and joints, as well as the circulation of blood and the disposition of blood vessels.[5] Ayala notes that the details Paley provided in *Natural Theology* represent the best science of his day, and that he went well beyond most of his contemporaries. Students of philosophy who are first introduced to Paley's design argument often overlook this point. Perhaps this is because most philosophy textbooks only include his famous watchmaker passage, where he writes,

> In crossing a heath, suppose I pitched my foot against a *stone*, and were asked how the stone came to be there, I might possibly answer, that, for any thing I knew to the contrary, it had lain there for ever: nor would it perhaps be very easy to show the absurdity of this answer. But suppose I had found a *watch* upon the ground, and it should be enquired how the watch happened to be in that place, I should hardly think of the answer which I had before given, that, for any thing I knew, the watch might have always been there.[6]

This passage provides a simple illustration of design detection, since it invites readers to reflect on the various distinctions between stones and watches. In doing so, one is able to recognize notable characteristics that exist in the watch but are absent in the stone. Paley walks his readers through this reflection by highlighting that a watch has "several parts

---

5. Ayala, "Darwin and Intelligent Design," 752-53. Ayala writes, "Paley was not the only proponent of the argument from design in Britain in the first half of the nineteenth century. A few years after the publication of *Natural Theology*, the eighth Earl of Bridgewater endowed the publication of treatises that would set forth 'the Power, Wisdom and Goodness of God as manifested in the Creation.' Eight treatises were published during 1833-40, several of which artfully incorporate the best science of the time and had considerable influence on the public and among scientists. William Buckland, professor of geology at Oxford University, notes in *Geology and Mineralogy* (1836) the world distribution of coal and mineral ores and proceeds to point out that they had been deposited in a remote part, yet obviously with the forethought of serving the larger human populations that would come about much later. Another geologist, Hugh Miller in *The Testimony of the Rocks* (1858), would argue that it is not only the perfection of design but also the beauty of natural structures found in rock formations and in mountains and rivers that manifests the intervention of the Creator" (Ayala, "Darwin and Intelligent Design," 753). Elsewhere Ayala notes other thinkers who embraced or promoted design arguments shortly before Paley, such as Henry More (1614-1687), Robert Hooke (1635-1703), Thomas Burnet (1635-1703), Bernard Nieuwentijdt (1654-1718), and even François Marie Arouet de Voltaire (1694-1778). Henry More, for example, argued that the succession of day and night provides a sign of divine design. Ayala, "No Place for Intelligent Design," 367.

6. Paley, *Natural Theology*, 7.

[that] are framed and put together for a purpose," whereas a stone has no such arrangements.[7]

Paley's watchmaker analogy is straightforward, but Ayala stresses that Paley's case is considerably more powerful when one reviews the numerous examples and elaborate details that Paley incorporates into his overall argument.[8] The paragraph below, for example, illustrates how Paley builds his case for design. He explains,

> I know no better method of introducing so large a subject, than that of comparing a single thing with a single thing; an eye, for example, with a telescope. As far as the examination of the instrument goes, there is precisely the same proof that the eye was made for vision, as there is that the telescope was made for assisting it. They are made upon the same principles; both being adjusted to the laws by which the transmission and refraction of rays of light are regulated. . . . For instance, these laws require, in order to produce the same effect, that the rays of light, in passing from water into the eye, should be refracted by a more convex surface than when it passes out of air into the eye. Accordingly we find that the eye of a fish, in that part of it called the crystalline lens, is much rounder than the eye of terrestrial animals. What plainer manifestation of design can there be than this difference? What could a mathematical instrument maker have done more to show his knowledge of this principle, his application of that knowledge, his suiting of his means to his end . . . to testify counsel, choice, consideration, [and] purpose?[9]

When considering the physiology of sight, Paley notes the differences between the eyes of terrestrial animals and the eyes of a fish. He reasons that the relevant differences manifest design, since there is a seemingly inexplicable correlation between how terrestrial eyes and fish eyes are each suited for their respective environments.

Paley additionally develops principles to clarify how our intuitions of design can be objectively articulated. He does this by comparing the creative powers of *chance* with the creative powers of *design*:

> What does chance ever do for us? In the human body, for instance, chance, that is, the operation of causes without design, may

---

7. Paley, *Natural Theology*, 7.

8. To demonstrate the force of Paley's argument, Ayala provides several lengthy passages of Paley's *Natural Theology*. See Ayala, "From Paley to Darwin," 59–62.

9. Paley, *Natural Theology*, 16.

produce a wen, a wart, a mole, a pimple, but never an eye. Among inanimate substances, a clod, a pebble, a liquid drop might be; but never was a watch, a telescope, an organized body of any kind, answering a valuable purpose by a complicated mechanism, the effect of chance. In no assignable instance has such a thing existed without intention somewhere.[10]

Chance, for Paley, is defined as the "operation of causes without design." It has the power to produce wens, warts, moles, and pimples, but such features have no recognizable purpose. An eye, however, does have a recognizable purpose. Eyes are designed for sight. Warts are not designed for anything. These distinctions are clear for Paley. Later, he expounds,

> When several different parts contribute to one effect, or, which is the same thing, when an effect is produced by the joint action of different instruments, the fitness of such parts or instruments to one another for the purpose of producing, by their united action, the effect, is what I call relation; and whenever this is observed in the works of nature or of man, it appears to me to carry along with it decisive evidence of understanding, intention, art . . . all depending upon the motions within, all upon the system of intermediate actions.[11]

Ayala highlights this passage in one of his articles, and then draws a parallel between what he calls "Paley's relation argument" and Michael Behe's argument for irreducible complexity (IC).[12] The argument, simply stated, maintains that various interconnected parts, which produce a single function when combined as a unit, could not arise by chance. Thus design is the only viable explanation for such occurrences.

Ayala appreciates the force of this argument, and he understands why Paley's contemporaries found it persuasive—noting that even Darwin was impressed.[13] After Darwin published *The Origin of Species*, however, Ayala claims that teleological explanations became irrelevant for science.[14] In fact,

---

10. Paley, *Natural Theology*, 38.
11. Paley, *Natural Theology*, 140.
12. Ayala, "From Paley to Darwin," 61.
13. In a letter written to John Lubbock, Darwin states, "I do not think I ever admired a book more than Paley's *Natural Theology*: I could almost formerly have said it by heart" (Darwin, *Origin of Species*, xxxi–xxxii).
14. Ayala argues that the motivating objective of Darwin's *Origin of Species* "was to provide a solution to Paley's problem; namely, to demonstrate how his discovery of natural selection would account for the design of organisms, without the need to resort to

that was Darwin's great accomplishment—to provide a scientific explanation of design.[15] He did this by presumably demonstrating that natural selection working on variations within organisms has the power to create seemingly designed features. Such features, therefore, are not *intelligently* designed but *naturally* designed. Ayala explains, "Darwin accepted that organisms are 'designed' for certain purposes; that is, they are functionally organized. Organisms are adapted to certain ways of life and their parts are designed to perform certain functions. Birds have wings for flying, fish have gills to breathe in water and trees have leaves to capture the sunlight."[16] Darwin's great idea thus introduced a new category for explaining the design of complex structures, namely, the category of *functional* design.

For Ayala, the functional organization of structures that arise because of natural selection is sufficient to explain Paley's various examples of design, including his complex descriptions of mammalian eyes. Though counterintuitive, Darwin's insights propose that gradual changes that accumulate over time, guided by natural selection, can eventually produce such complexities. Paley knew nothing about this kind of mechanism, which is why he was unable to imagine any alternative to design. Darwin explains,

> To suppose that the eye, with all its inimitable contrivances for adjusting the focus to different distances, for admitting different amounts of light, and for the correction of spherical and chromatic aberration, could have been formed by natural selection, seems, I freely confess, absurd in the highest possible degree. Yet reason tells me, that if numerous gradations from a perfect and complex eye to one very imperfect and simple, each grade being useful to its possessor, can be shown to exist; if further, the eye does vary ever so slightly, and the variations be inherited, which is certainly the case; and if any variation or modification in the organ be ever useful to an animal under changing conditions of life, then the difficulty of believing that a perfect and complex eye could be formed by natural selection, though insuperable by our imagination, can hardly be considered real.[17]

---

supernatural agencies" (Ayala, "From Paley to Darwin," 67).

15. Ayala, *Big Questions*, 47. Scientific explanations, for Ayala, are nonteleological explanations.

16. Ayala, *Big Questions*, 16.

17. Darwin, *Origin of Species*, 140. Darwin further writes, "It is scarcely possible to avoid comparing the eye to a telescope. We know that this instrument has been perfected by the long continued efforts of the highest human intellects; and we naturally infer that the eye has been formed by a somewhat analogous process. But may not this inference

Ayala argues that Darwin's aforementioned insights highlight the fatal flaw in the structure of Paley's argument. That is, Paley only refers to *chance* and *design* when articulating the modes of causation in biology. Darwin, however, introduces a third category when he articulates his theory of natural selection. Moreover, Darwin draws out two important implications after introducing this third category. First, *chance* variations and *natural selection* can work together to produce innovative changes in organisms. When this happens, one should recognize that complex structures originate through a selective (rather than a random) process. Second, this selective process has the power to build over time, which means that natural selection working on chance variations has a greater capacity to explain high degrees of complexity. Thus the designs of eye-like structures are far more explicable from a naturalistic perspective.

The General Case for Evolution

Given Darwin's insights mentioned above, Ayala finds it astonishing that modern thinkers still promote ideas like ID and question the validity of biological evolution. He assumes this happens because the public is, broadly speaking, scientifically illiterate. For this reason, he frequently assures his general readers that the evidence for evolution has been so substantiated that professional scientists no longer debate whether it happened. He writes, "scientists agree that the evolutionary origin of animals and plants is a scientific conclusion beyond reasonable doubt. They place it beside such established concepts as the roundness of the Earth, its rotation around the Sun, and the molecular composition of matter."[18] Debates surrounding the evidence and arguments for ID and evolution, therefore, do not happen within the scientific community according to Ayala. Biologists already consider evolution a fact, so there is no need to discuss the arguments and evidence for ID.[19]

---

be presumptuous? Have we any right to assume that the Creator works by intellectual power like those of man? If we must compare the eye to an optical instrument, we ought in imagination to take a thick layer of transparent tissue, with a nerve sensitive to light beneath, and then suppose every part of this layer to be continually changing slowly in density, so as to separate into layers of different densities and thicknesses, placed at different distances from each other, and with the surfaces of each layer slowly changing in form" (Darwin, *Origin of Species*, 141).

18. Ayala, "Darwin and Intelligent Design," 760.
19. Ayala, *Big Questions*, 17.

Ayala's confidence brings up important questions regarding the definition of evolution. He boldly asserts that the evidence for evolution is overwhelming, but what precisely does he mean by evolution? In several places, he articulates answers to this question. First, he describes evolution as "the modern theory of evolution, or the synthetic theory of evolution."[20] By this, he means a theory of evolution that combines Mendelian genetics with Darwinian natural selection, which promotes three basic ideas:[21]

1. Hereditary variations occur, some more favorable than others to the organisms.

2. More organisms are produced than can possibly survive and reproduce.

3. Organisms with more favorable variations will survive and reproduce more successfully.

Ayala asserts that two consequences follow from these three ideas. The first consequence is that organisms that adapt to their environment will have a higher chance of living and reproducing. This consequence is both obvious and well documented within the natural world. The second consequence is that changes will occur and build on each other over time. Again, this consequence is obvious and well documented in the natural world. If one accepts these three ideas, followed by the two consequences, then one accepts the modern theory of biological evolution. Ayala finds it surprising, therefore, that such a simple and obvious idea would be controversial.

Of course, Ayala's simple portrayal of evolution deemphasizes aspects of evolution that makes it controversial. He is certainly correct to describe the synthetic theory of evolution as descent with modification. But he also knows that evolution is a far more expansive theory, which includes the additional notion that all organisms "are related by descent from common ancestors."[22] This more expansive claim is significantly different than mere descent with modification. Even so, Ayala maintains that common ancestry is just as established as descent with modification, though he does make three critical distinctions between the *fact of evolution*, the *history of evolution*, and the *mechanisms of evolution*.[23] The *fact of evolution* is the

20. Ayala, "Evolution of Life," 65.
21. Cela-Conde and Ayala, *Human Evolution*, 1–4.
22. Ayala, *Am I a Monkey?*, 18.
23. Ayala, *Am I a Monkey?*, 20. Ayala's threefold definition of evolution corresponds to Dembski and Wells's twofold definition of evolution. They explain that evolution is "a

notion that all organisms share a common ancestor. This notion, according to Ayala, is not controversial among scientists. The *history of evolution* and the *mechanisms of evolution*, on the other hand, do evoke legitimate debates and are therefore "matters of active scientific investigation."[24] When Ayala references the *history of evolution*, he is referring to disagreements regarding when lineages split from one another. When he refers to the *mechanism of evolution*, he refers to scientific debates concerning the precise processes that drive evolutionary development.[25] While the *history of evolution* and the *mechanism of evolution* evoke debate, Ayala stresses that such debates

---

claim about natural history and is known as 'common descent' or 'universal common ancestry.' According to it, there is a common ancestor to which all living organisms trace their lineage. [They also] assert that evolutionary change proceeds by purely material mechanisms and thus requires no intelligent guidance. Intelligence, on this view, is a product of evolution rather than something that guides it" (Dembski and Wells, *Design of Life*, xxi). Elsewhere, Dembski writes, "Evolution can be construed as a fully naturalistic, purposeless process that by means of natural selection and mutation has produced all living things. On the other hand, evolution can mean nothing more than organisms have changed over time" (Dembski, "What Every Theologian Should Know," 232). Alvin Plantinga offers yet a more detailed definition of evolution. He mentions that the term frequently refers to six distinct claims: (1) the *ancient earth thesis*, or the claim that the earth is 4.5 billion years old; (2) it can refer to the *progress thesis*, the claim that life has progressed from relatively simple to relatively complex forms; (3) it can refer to *descent with modification*. This is the claim that the "enormous diversity of the contemporary living world has come about by way of offspring differing, ordinarily in small and subtle ways, from their parents"; (4) it can refer to the *common ancestry thesis*, which states that life originated at only one place on earth, and all subsequent life is related by descent to those original living creatures; (5) it can refer to *Darwinism*, which for Plantinga is the claim that there is a naturalistic mechanism driving the process of descent with modification; and (6) it can refer to the *naturalistic origins thesis*. This is the idea that "life itself developed from non-living matter without any special creative activity of God but just by virtue of processes described by the ordinary laws of physics and chemistry" (Plantinga, *Where the Conflict Really Lies*, 8–10).

24. Ayala, *Am I a Monkey?*, 21.

25. These processes include random mutation and natural selection, and other proposals such as population genetics, genetic drift, evolutionary development (evo-devo), gene flow, punctuated equilibrium, etc.

do not undermine the *fact of evolution*.[26] His first task in undermining ID, then, is to demonstrate the *fact of evolution*.[27]

Ayala begins this task by explaining the fossil record and biogeography for his readers. He claims that the fossil record demonstrates that life evolved in a haphazard fashion, rather than in an orderly or designed fashion. He explains,

> The radiations of some groups of organisms, the numerical and territorial expansions of other groups, the replacement of some kinds of organisms by other kinds, the occasional but irregular occurrence of trends toward increased size or other sorts of chance, and the ever-present extinctions are best explained by natural selection of organisms subject to the vagaries of genetic mutation, environmental challenge, and past history. The scientific account of these events does not necessitate recourse to a preordained plan, whether imprinted from the beginning or through successive interventions by an omniscient and almighty Designer. Biological evolution differs from a painting or an artifact in that it is not the outcome of preconceived design. The design of organisms is not intelligent, but imperfect and, at times, outright dysfunctional.[28]

For Ayala, the fossil record both confirms *the fact of evolution* and disconfirms ID. This is because ID, according to Ayala, makes significantly different predictions than *the fact of evolution*. Intelligent design presumably leads to a hypothesis that can be tested by examining the fossil record. That is, if the world of biology is best explained by an intelligent designer, then one would expect to see a certain degree of perfection, intentional planning, or order when examining the fossil evidence. The reality of extinction and the replacement of some kinds of organisms by other kinds, however, suggest that life is not the result of a preordained plan.

---

26. He writes, "It seems unlikely that theories as extensively corroborated by contributions from so many disciplines as the evolution of organisms will ever be rejected or replaced. Surely, however, the theory of evolution will be further developed and advanced" (Ayala, *Am I a Monkey?*, 24). He further references the fact that the overwhelming majority of biologists embrace evolution, and notes that the evidence "no longer engages the interest of biologists except when explaining evolution to the public or arguing with those who refuse to accept evolution" (Ayala, *Am I a Monkey?*, 49–50).

27. In the body of this chapter, I demonstrate that the evidence for common ancestry is irrelevant when it comes to the debate over ID. While ID advocates are split regarding whether all life originated from a common ancestor, they all agree that the cogency of ID is not contingent upon the question of common ancestry.

28. Ayala, "No Place for Intelligent Design," 382.

By highlighting imperfections within the fossil record, Ayala reframes the supposed problem of the fossil record promoted by many evolutionary critics. Critics of evolution often claim that a close examination of the fossil record demonstrates that there is a lack of transitional fossils. Darwin himself noted this problem in *The Origin of Species* when he wrote, "Why, if species have descended from other species by insensible fine gradations, do we not everywhere see innumerable transitional forms?"[29] Dembski and Wells, in fact, refer to this quote by Darwin and offer the following critique of *the fact of evolution*:

> To his credit, Darwin acknowledged that this absence of transitional forms created a serious problem for his theory. Nonetheless, despite this acknowledgement, many scientists continued to find his case for evolution compelling. Perhaps, they reasoned, the missing transitional fossils would eventually be found. In Darwin's day, fossil findings were patchy and the search itself was unsystematic. Darwin himself hoped that the missing transitional forms would turn up as scientists searched more deliberately and systematically. Thus began the search for "missing links." What did paleontologists find? Many new fossils, to be sure. But what they didn't find were the numerous intermediates that, according to Darwin's theory, had once existed.[30]

This passage is important to consider when evaluating Ayala's scientific case against ID. As two prominent ID advocates, Dembski and Wells are challenging *the fact of evolution* by appealing to the fossil record. One might conclude, therefore, that ID and *the fact of evolution* are two opposing positions. A close examination of the entire ID movement, however, shows that such a conclusion is a mistake. Some ID advocates challenge *the fact of evolution*, whereas others embrace it. I will address this issue in detail

---

29. Darwin, *Origin of Species*, 129. Of course, Darwin provided a response to this question and devoted a whole chapter to explaining the lack of evidence. He writes, "I believe the answer mainly lies in the record being incomparably less perfect than is generally supposed; the imperfection of the record being chiefly due to organic being not inhabiting profound depths of the sea, and to their remains being embedded and preserved to a future age only in masses of sediment sufficiently thick and extensive to withstand an enormous amount of future degradation; and such fossiliferous masses can be accumulated only where much sediment is deposited on the shallow bed of the sea, whilst it slowly subsides" (Darwin, *Origin of Species*, 130). Since Darwin, paleontologists have amassed a numerous fossils that allegedly confirm Darwin's theory. I discuss the more noteworthy discoveries later in this section.

30. Dembski and Wells, *Design of Life*, 61–62.

later, but I briefly mention it now to help guide our evaluation of Ayala's scientific critique of ID.

Contra Dembski and Wells, Ayala claims that intermediates are now abundant and that the fossil record clearly shows an evolutionary progression of life. Ayala provides an overview of this evidence, beginning with the earliest known fossils—dated to 3.4 billion years old. These early fossils are simple and resemble microorganisms such as bacteria.[31] After simple prokaryotic cells appear in the fossil record, one finds eukaryotic cells dating approximately to 2.0 billion years old. This shows a progression from simple life to more complex life as time progresses. Ayala explains that this progression continues throughout the fossil record. He writes,

> The oldest known animal fossils, nearly 700 million years old, come from the Ediacara fauna, small wormlike creatures with soft bodies. Numerous fossils belonging to many animal phyla and exhibiting mineralized skeletons appear in rocks about 540 million years old, during the geological period known as the Cambrian. (A phylum, plural phyla, is a major group of organisms, such as the molluscs or the chordates.) These organisms are different from those living now and from those living at intervening times. Some are so radically different that paleontologists have had to create new phyla in order to classify them. The first vertebrates (phylum Chordata, or chordates) appeared more than 400 million years ago; the first mammals less than 200 million years ago. The history of life recorded by fossils presents compelling evidence of evolution.[32]

To offer a visual of this progression, Ayala provides the following table:[33]

Life Form	Millions of Years Since First Known Appearance
Microbial (prokaryotic cells)	3,500
Complex (eukaryotic cells)	1,400–2,000
First multicellular animals	670
Shell-bearing animals	540

31. Ayala, *Big Questions*, 121.
32. Ayala, *Big Questions*, 121.
33. Ayala, *Big Questions*, 122.

A SCIENTIFIC CRITIQUE OF DESIGN IN BIOLOGY

Life Form	Millions of Years Since First Known Appearance
Vertebrates (simple fishes)	490
Amphibians	350
Reptiles	310
Mammals	200
Non-human primates	60
Earliest apes	25
Australopithecine ancestors	5
Homo sapiens (modern humans)	0.15 (150,000 years)

Referring to this table, Ayala explains that the particular order of the fossil record demonstrates common ancestry. And if common ancestry is accepted, he further explains that one can make predictions regarding future paleontological discoveries. For example, amphibians will likely never appear before fish, mammals will never appear before reptiles, and complex life will never appear before the oldest eukaryotic cells.[34] These predictions are repeatedly confirmed, and thus Ayala insists that common ancestry is the most plausible interpretation of the fossil record.[35]

After explaining the basic order of the fossil record, Ayala shifts to the problem of transitional fossils. As mentioned above, Ayala disagrees with Dembski and Wells regarding the evidence for transitional fossils. He claims there are intermediate fossils between fish and amphibians, amphibians and reptiles, and between reptiles and mammals. These fossils, for

---

34. Ayala, *Big Questions*, 123.

35. Ayala briefly considers the notion that all the fossils were deposited in a worldwide flood, as proposed by young earth creationists. Concerning this idea, he writes, "There is clear evidence in the form of inter-tidal and terrestrial deposits that at no recorded time in the past has the entire planet been under water. Moreover, a universal flood of sufficient magnitude to deposit the existing strata, which together are many scores of kilometres thick, would require a volume of water far greater than has ever existed on and in the Earth, at least since the formation of the first known solid crust about four billion years ago. The belief that all this sediment with its fossils was deposited in an orderly sequence in only a year defies all geological observations and physical principles. There were periods of unusually high rainfall, and extensive flooding of inhabited areas has occurred, but there is no scientific support for the hypothesis of a universal mountain-topping flooding" (Ayala, *Big Questions*, 123).

Ayala, are so numerous that it is "often difficult to identify categorically where the transition occurs from one to another particular genus or from one to another particular species."[36] He focuses particularly on two alleged intermediates that often receive media attention, namely, *Archaeopteryx* and *Tiktaalik*. *Archaeopteryx* is commonly recognized as an intermediate between reptiles and birds.[37] Paleontologists regularly highlight that *Archaeopteryx*'s skeleton is reptile-like, and yet the fossils indicates that it also had feathers. The skull of *Archaeopteryx* is bird-like with an expanded braincase, large eye sockets, a pronounced beak, teeth (unlike modern birds), and may have been capable of flying.[38]

Ayala also mentions *Tiktaalik*. This fossil was discovered in 2004, and first published in 2006. The *Tiktaalik* fossil is commonly recognized as an intermediate between fish and tetrapods, and Ayala describes it as a flattened, superficially crocodile-like animal. He continues his description:

> [*Tiktaalik's*] fish-like features include small pelvic fins, fin rays rather than digits in their paired appendages, and well-developed gill arches, which suggest that they remained mostly aquatic. But the bony gill cover has disappeared, indicating reduced water flow through the gill chamber. The elongated snout suggests a shift from sucking toward snapping up pray, mostly on land. The relatively large ribs indicate that *Tiktaalik* could support its body out of water.[39]

---

36. Ayala, *Big Questions*, 122.

37. Dembski and Wells consider the case of *Archaeopteryx* in *The Design of Life*, and are not convinced that it represents a compelling transitional form. They write, "The feathers in *Archaeopteryx* appear to be identical to those in modern birds, having the structure of a genuine airfoil. Yet, in place of the standard adaptational package characteristic of birds, Archaeopteryx has several reptilian features, including a bony tail, teeth in its beak and claws on its wings. The case of the duck-billed platypus is similar. The platypus lays eggs and has a bill like a duck. But except for these bird-like features, it is like other mammals in possessing fur and suckling its young. Taxonomists classify it as a mammal, and it has never been considered a transitional form between birds and mammals. Most proposed missing links are like this—rather than merging taxonomic groups, they fall almost exclusively in one group or another" (Dembski and Wells, *Design of Life*, 62).

38. Ayala, *Darwin and Intelligent Design*, 33. Ayala notes that the first *Archaeopteryx* fossil was discovered in Bavaria in 1861, and since then there have been many *Archaeopteryx* discoveries (the most recent discovery appeared in December 2005).

39. Ayala, *Darwin and Intelligent Design*, 32.

Before the *Tiktaalik* discovery, Ayala notes that *Panderichthys* was the closest known fish fossil to the tetrapods. The earliest known tetrapod fossils were *Ichthyostega* and *Acanthostega*.[40] As science progresses, consequently, Ayala suspects that the purported gaps will continue to close.

Archaeopteryx and *Tiktaalik* are undoubtedly important fossils to examine, but even if they are appropriately classified as transitional fossils, they do not seem to challenge the central notion of ID. As mentioned above, however, this does not mean that all ID advocates acknowledge such fossils as intermediates. In *The Design of Life*, Dembski and Wells offer several critiques of alleged transitional fossils. They claim that most proposed intermediates fall almost exclusively into one taxonomical group or another, but never as true intermediates.[41] They further insist that gaps in the fossil record persist, and that Darwinian advocates rarely consider alternative (teleological) interpretations of the available evidence. Broadly speaking, Dembski and Wells offer four possible interpretations that account for the purported gaps, namely:[42]

1. The Imperfect Record Interpretation. The gaps result from imperfections in the fossil record. Only a small fraction of the organisms that lived in the past have been preserved as fossils. It is therefore unlikely that future research will fill in the gaps. Support for the theory of evolution must look beyond the fossil record.

2. The Insufficient Search Interpretation. The gaps result from a failure to examine the fossil-bearing strata thoroughly enough. The gaps will close as a more complete sampling of fossils is taken.

3. The Punctuated Equilibrium Interpretation. The gaps result from evolution being a saltational or "jerky" process. Darwin was wrong about evolution being smooth and gradual. Evolution happens rapidly in small, isolated populations, punctuating an otherwise stagnant equilibrium. Although transitional forms must have existed, few, if any, get preserved.

4. The Abrupt Emergence Interpretation. The gaps are real and reflect fundamental discontinuities in nature. Basic groups of organisms

---

40. Ayala, *Big Questions*, 126. Interestingly, Dembski and Wells do not consider *Tiktaalik* in *Design of Life*. This is strange since *Design of Life* was published in 2009 and the discovery of *Tiktaalik* was published in 2006.
41. Dembski and Wells, *Design of Life*, 62.
42. Dembski and Wells, *Design of Life*, 69.

emerged suddenly. Transitional forms connecting these basic groups never existed.

According to Dembski and Wells, the fourth option (abrupt emergence) is the face-value interpretation of the available evidence.[43] The first three options, they explain, are justified more by methodological naturalism (MN), a philosophical position, than by the actual fossil evidence. And since they reject MN, they maintain that abrupt emergence is the more plausible interpretation of the data.[44] The overall project of ID, however, is not dependent upon Dembski and Wells being correct on this issue.

The next line of evidence for common ancestry offered by Ayala comes from comparative anatomy. He describes and provides images of various skeletons to show the striking similarities between different creatures. Ayala argues that such similarities insinuate and are consistent with the idea that each fossil shares a common ancestor. Of course, a common response to this idea is that morphological similarities indicate a common designer rather than a common ancestor. Dembski and Wells elaborate on this type of counterargument:

> In a 1990 book intended to refute critics of Darwinian evolution, biologist Tim Berra used pictures of various models of Corvette automobiles to illustrate how the fossil record provides evidence for descent with modification. "If you compare a 1953 and a 1954 Corvette, side by side," he wrote, "then a 1954 and a 1955 model, and so on, the descent with modification is overwhelmingly obvious." But automobiles are designed, not descended from other automobiles. Berra actually proved the opposite of what he intended, namely, that a series of similarities could be a product of intelligent design rather than Darwinian evolution.[45]

---

43. Dembski and Wells, *Design of Life*, 77.

44. Dembski and Wells further explain that there are four ways to understand abrupt emergence, namely, "(1) Nonbiogenic formation. Organisms form without the direct causal agency of other organisms. In place of life begetting life, here we have nonlife begetting life; (2) symbiogenic reorganization. Organisms emerge when different organisms from different species come together and reorganize themselves into new organisms; (3) biogenic reinvention—organisms reinvent themselves in midstream. At one moment they have certain morphological and genetic features, at the next they have vastly different set of such features. (4) Generative transmutation. Organisms, in reproducing, produce offspring that are vastly different from themselves" (Dembski and Wells, *Design of Life*, 78).

45. Dembski and Wells, *Design of Life*, 88.

Ayala argues that this common-designer counterargument is misguided. From a purely practical point of view, he explains, "it seems incomprehensible that a turtle and a whale should swim, a horse run, a person write, and a bird or bat fly with forelimb structures built of the same bones."[46] Engineers do not simply re-tweak parts from one system and retool them for another system. An engineer would develop totally new parts that were designed specifically for the needed functions. If we accept the idea that every organism had a common ancestor, then similarities of structures make sense.[47] If we accept the idea of design, however, it becomes more challenging to understand why similar parts are retooled for different functions.[48]

To provide additional support to the common ancestry interpretation of morphological similarities, Ayala explicates the evidence from embryonic development and vestiges. He explains,

---

46. Ayala, *Darwin and Intelligent Design*, 34. Ayala also writes, "Why are our arms and our legs, which are used for such different functions, made of the same materials, the same bones, muscles, and nerves, all arranged in the same overall pattern? Evolution makes sense of the anomaly. Our remote ancestors' forelimbs were legs. After our ancestors became bipedal and started using their forelimbs for functions other than walking, these became gradually modified but retained their original composition and arrangement. Engineers start with raw materials and a design suited for a particular purpose; evolution can only modify what is already there. An engineer who would design both cars and airplanes, or both wings and wheels, using the same materials arranged in a similar pattern, would surely be fired" (Ayala, "From Paley to Darwin," 65). ID advocates recognize this phenomenon as well. Dembski and Wells acknowledge, "Similarity of structure and divergence of function is common. For instance, the pattern of bones in a bat's wing is similar to that in a porpoise's flipper, though the wing is used for flying and the flipper is used for swimming" (Dembski and Wells, *Design of Life*, 117).

47. Ayala, *Big Questions*, 19.

48. Although there are design analogies from computer programing that might make sense of this data from an ID perspective. In 2018, I brought up this retooling problem to Winston Ewert during a session on Evolutionary Informatics at the CSC Seminar on Intelligent Design in the Natural Sciences—hosted by Discovery Institute in Seattle, WA. Ewert's lecture and response to my question provided new ways of thinking about design in nature. If one thinks of design only in terms of simple engineering, then the retooling problem seems significant when studying comparative anatomy. If one thinks of design in terms of computer programming, however, then the retooling problem can be seen as an example of simple recoding. Computer programmers, from what I can tell, frequently use similar lines of code to produce different functions. Perhaps computer programming, then, provides a better analogy for understanding design within living systems. Changes made at the genetic level would be analogous to codes recreated by programmers, and thus changes at the phenotypic level would be analogous to the functions brought about by such recoding. For more information on the relevance of computer programming to evolution and ID, see Marks II, Dembski and Ewert, *Introduction to Evolutionary Informatics*.

> The embryos of humans and other non-aquatic vertebrates exhibit gill slits even though they never breathe through gills. These slits are found in the embryos of all vertebrates because they share as common ancestors the fish in which these structures first evolved. Human embryos also exhibit, by the fourth week of development, a well-defined tail, which reaches its maximum length at six weeks. Similar embryonic tails are found in other mammals, such as dogs, horses, and monkeys; in humans, however, the tail eventually shortens, persisting only as a rudiment in the adult coccyx. Embryonic rudiments are inconsistent with claims of intelligent design: why would a structure be designed to form during early development if it will disappear before birth?[49]

In this paragraph, Ayala continues to develop the idea that evidence for common ancestry provides evidence against ID. His assumption is that a designer would not create (or allow) situations where early stages of embryonic development form structures that seem superfluous during later stages.[50] Vestiges illustrate this point for Ayala, because he considers them instances of imperfections that negate the idea of design.[51]

While the evidence mentioned above is enough to convince Ayala of the *fact of evolution*, he argues that the most conclusive evidence comes from molecular biology.[52] He explains,

> The virtually unlimited evolutionary information encoded in the DNA sequence of living organisms allows evolutionists to reconstruct any evolutionary relationships that have led to present-day organisms, or among them, with as much detail as wanted. Invest the necessary resources (time and laboratory expenses), and you can have the answer to any query with as much precision as you want.[53]

---

49. Ayala, *Big Questions*, 22.

50. He also seems to assume that ID necessarily rejects all forms of evolutionary development. I demonstrate in chapter 4 that this assumption is incorrect.

51. Ayala, *Darwin and Intelligent Design*, 36. Contra Ayala, Dembski and Wells argue, "Vestigial structures are entirely consistent with intelligent design, suggesting structures that were initially designed but then lost their function through disuse" (Dembski and Wells, *Design of Life*, 133). Later they argue, "[Vestiges] are entirely consistent with evolution as a process directed by a designing intelligence. Bottom line: vestigiality does not make the design problem go away" (Dembski and Wells, *Design of Life*, 136).

52. Ayala, *Darwin and Intelligent Design*, 37.

53. Ayala, "Molecular Evolution," 132.

Molecular biology, therefore, makes it possible to reconstruct the entire tree of life.[54] This makes any alleged gap in the fossil record irrelevant, and it confirms various predictions made by the common ancestry thesis. Ayala conveys the molecular evidence in great detail, and is worth quoting at length:

> The molecular components of organisms are remarkably uniform in the nature of the components, as well as in the ways in which they are assembled and used. In all bacteria, archaea, plants, animals, and humans, the DNA consists of a different sequence of the same four component nucleotides (represented as A, C, G, and T). The genetic code, by which the information contained in the DNA of the cell nucleus is passed on to proteins, is virtually the same in all organisms.... This unity reveals the genetic continuity and common ancestry of all organisms. There is no other rational way to account for their molecular uniformity when numerous alternative structures are in principle equally likely. The genetic code serves as an example. Each particular sequence of three nucleotides in the nuclear DNA acts as a pattern for the production of exactly the same amino acid in all organisms. This is no more necessary than it is for a language to use a particular combination of letters to represent a particular object.[55]

Ayala illustrates the persuasiveness of this evidence by considering what it would be like to compare two similar books to one another. He explains,

> Both books are 200 pages long and contain the same number of chapters. Closer examination reveals that the two books are identical page for page and word for word, except that an occasional word—say, 1 in 100—is different. The two books cannot have been written independently; either one has been copied from the other, or both have been copied, directly or indirectly, from the

---

54. Dembski and Wells disagree on this point. They write, "Molecular phylogeny has failed, utterly and completely, to establish that universal common ancestry is true. It has failed to provide reliable dating for, much less chronicle, the history of life. It has failed to specify what evolutionary relationships, if any, exist among living forms. And it has failed, spectacularly, to given an unambiguous indication of what the universal common ancestor—if there even was one—might have looked like. Was it an organism, a group of organisms, or a batch of chemicals? The molecular evidence for common ancestry, like the fossil and embryo evidence is plagued with inconsistencies and unanswered questions. In fact, Darwinism must be *assumed* in order to explain the evidence" (Dembski and Wells, *Design of Life*, 131).

55. Ayala, "Molecular Evolution," 133.

same original book. In living beings, if each component nucleotide of DNA is represented by one letter, the complete sequence of nucleotides in the DNA of a higher organism would require several hundred books, each with hundreds of pages, with several thousand letters on each page. When the "pages" (or sequences of nucleotides) in these "books" (genomes) are examined one by one, the correspondence in the "letters" (nucleotides) gives unmistakable evidence of common origin.[56]

This book analogy provides two arguments for common ancestry according to Ayala. The first argument focuses on the fact that both books are written in the same language. This suggests that both books, at a basic level, have a common language origin. The second argument focuses on each individual character. If each character is virtually identical (with just a few random mistakes), then one would reasonably discern that each book has a specific common origin. When it comes to the evidence from DNA, Ayala's book analogy is appropriate. If two organisms have virtually identical DNA (character-by-character), then one can reasonably assume that they originated from a common source. While ID advocates contend that the common source originates from a common designer, Ayala contends that the evidence supports the notion of common ancestry.[57]

Ayala's case for common ancestry is compelling, although there is a missing link in his argument. That is, he does not draw a clear connection between how evidence for common ancestry negates the scientific project of ID. Even though Dembski and Wells argue against common ancestry, they still grant that there is no scientific conflict between affirming both common ancestry and ID.[58] The major conflict between evolution and ID

---

56. Ayala, "Molecular Evolution," 135–36.

57. Ayala, "Molecular Evolution," 136. These two ideas are not necessarily mutually exclusive, as will be demonstrated when examining Dembski's work.

58. One could argue that there is a theological critique between common ancestry and the biblical doctrine of creation, but this is an entirely different argument. Strictly speaking, ID (as a scientific position) does not take a stance on common ancestry. Dembski and Wells write, "It's important here not to get caught in a false dilemma. A false dilemma presents a choice between two options, neither of which is entirely acceptable, but which together purport to be mutually exclusive and exhaustive. The false dilemma here is common design versus common ancestry. It's logically possible to have common design without common ancestry and common ancestry without common design. But common design and common ancestry are not mutually exclusive. The two can work together. We can think of life consisting of hierarchically arranged design modules that over the course of natural history have sustained substantial evolutionary change through the activity of natural forces as well as through the guidance of a

centers more on the proposed *mechanisms of evolution*, and Ayala admits there are legitimate debates on that matter.[59]

Evidence for Human Evolution

The third step in Ayala's case against ID includes a general argument for human evolution. This is perhaps a strategic step for Ayala, since arguably the main religious complaint with evolution is the notion that humans share a lineage with lower animals. From a theological perspective, particularly, there is a conceivable conflict between human evolution and the Judeo-Christian doctrine of the *imago Dei*.[60] Because of this conflict, Ayala apparently needs

---

supervising intelligence. Just how much evolutionary change has occurred in each way remains an open question" (Dembski and Wells, *Design of Life*, 142). Behe also affirms common ancestry. He writes, "I find the idea of common descent (that all organisms share a common ancestor) fairly convincing, and have no particular reason to doubt it" (Behe, *Darwin's Black Box*, 5).

59. More precisely, the debate is over which modes of causation are allowed in discussions about biology. When discussing mutations as a mechanism, for example, an ID advocate might embrace *chance* mutations and/or *designed* mutations. From Ayala's perspective, however, only *chance* mutations are considered legitimate for science. Thus the debate centers on whether *design* is an appropriate mode of causation more than whether ID advocates are can propose an alternative mechanism.

60. I mention that there is a *conceivable conflict* (rather than a necessary conflict) between human evolution and the doctrine of the *imago Dei*, but this issue is certainly debated among Christian theologians. My purpose is not to argue for a particular position, but only to highlight a potential reason why Ayala thinks the evidence for human evolution provides a counter to ID. At certain points, he seems to conflate ID with a *special creationist perspective* (Adam created from the dust 6,000-10,000 years ago) on the *imago Dei*. If he is not conflating the two, then I am not sure why he considers evidence for human evolution an additional critique of ID. Dembski and Wells agree when they write, "Regardless of whether one is a biblical creationist or an atheistic Darwinist or anything in between, all are agreed that humans did not magically materialize out of nothing. Humans arose from preexisting material stuff. Indeed, the very word 'human' refers to the earth (humus) that lies beneath our feet. In this respect, monkeys and humans are both modified dirt, and that is true regardless of whether humans are, in addition, modified monkeys. ID is compatible with each of these possibilities, and there are ID proponents who hold to each" (Dembski, and Wells, *Design of Life*, 21-22). Behe, additionally, agrees that humans are descendants of apes-like ancestors. He writes, "Evolution from a common ancestor, via changes in DNA, is *very* well supported. It may or may not be random. Thanks to evolution, scientists who sequence human DNA and find mutations that are helpful—against, say, our natural enemies—are not just studying the DNA of one person. They are actually observing the results of a struggle that's gone on for millennia and involved millions and millions of people. An ancestor of the modern human first sustained the helpful mutation, and her descendants outcompeted

to provide additional scientific arguments for human evolution to convince religious believers. If he succeeds in this task, then perhaps other ideas related to evolutionary biology will become easier to accept.[61]

Throughout Ayala's various works, he provides a detailed exposition of the evidence for human evolution. He explains that humans, from a scientific perspective, can be distinguished from other hominids by their ability to develop language and make complex tools. This distinction is detected in the fossil record when one examines the size of the cranium (called cranial capacity, or cc). Ayala notes, "The average cranial capacity of modern humans is 1,350 cc., while that of chimpanzees, with a comparable body size to ours, is 450 cc."[62] When investigating the fossil record, therefore, it is critical to measure the size of the cranium.

Ayala begins his survey of the fossil record with the oldest known fossil hominids, *Sahelanthropus* and *Orrorin*. These hominids are dated between six million to seven million years old. The next oldest is *Ardipithecus*, and is over four million years old. From there, paleontologists have discovered numerous *Australopithecus* fossils, dating from three million to four million years old. *Australopithecus* is noteworthy because it had an upright human stance, but also a smaller cranial capacity (500 cc, one-third the size of modern humans). The most famous *Australopithecus* discovery is Lucy (*Australopithecus afarensis*), which included 40 percent of her skeleton at a single site.

Contemporaries of *Australopithecus* were *Kenyanthropus* and *Paranthropus*, and *Homo habilis* appears in Africa just under two million years

---

the descendants of many other humans. So the modern situation reflects an evolutionary history involving many people" (Behe, *Edge of Evolution*, 12).

61. Note that this paragraph is mostly speculation on my part. I debated whether to include a section on human evolution in this chapter, since it did not seem entirely relevant to Ayala's case. In the end, however, I decided to include it since Ayala devotes a chapter to human evolution in *Darwin and Intelligent Design*. As mentioned in the footnote above, I think he does this because he conflates ID with a *special creationist perspective* on human origins. Elsewhere, he challenges this understanding of the *imago Dei* on scientific and theological grounds. He writes, "The Book of Genesis dramatically sets forth humans' lofty uniqueness within the natural world: 'So God created humankind in his image, in the image of God he created them; man and female he create them' (Gen 1:27). It does not take a great deal of biological expertise to realize that humans have organs and limbs similar to those of other animals; that we bear our young like other mammals; that, bone by bone, there is a precise correspondence between the skeletons of a chimpanzee and a human. But it does not take much reflection to notice the unique distinctiveness of our species" (Ayala, "Human Nature," 31).

62. Cela-Conde and Ayala, *Human Evolution*, 84.

ago (600 cc). Shortly after *Homo habilis* comes *Homo erectus* (800–1,100 cc). *Homo erectus* migrated out of Africa into Europe, Asia, the Middle East, Indonesia, and northern China. Between 500,000 years and 1.8 million years, *Homo ergaster, Homo antecessor,* and *Homo heidelbergensis* also appear in the fossil record. These three species all have cranial capacities similar to *Homo erectus.*

The transition to *Homo sapiens,* according to the fossil record, occurred around 400,000 years ago. The evidence suggests that *Homo sapiens* and *Homo erectus* lived together, since there are fossil remains of *Homo erectus* dating to 100,000 years ago in Java (Indonesia). *Homo neanderthalensis* is another species that is contemporary with *Homo sapiens,* and it appeared in Europe around 200,000 to 30,000 years ago. Many anthropologists argue that modern humans arose in Africa around 100,000 years ago.

As mentioned in the previous section, Ayala argues that the best evidence for evolution is the molecular evidence, and this is also true for human evolution.[63] After molecular biologists and geneticists completed the human genome project, Ayala explains that the evidence showed that in the genome regions shared by humans and chimpanzees, the two species are 99 percent identical. This means that there is a difference of about 30 million DNA letters out of the 3 billion letters in each genome.[64] Perhaps the most noteworthy genetic difference between humans and all other primates, however, is that humans have 23 pairs of chromosomes, whereas others have 24 pairs of chromosomes. From the perspective of common ancestry, Ayala suggests that this difference allows geneticists to make a prediction. He explains that somewhere in the human lineage, there must have been a mutation that caused two chromosomes to fuse in the human genome. If one could demonstrate that such a mutation did

---

63. When it comes to demonstrating that humans share a common ancestry with other primates, he explains that there are three ways to argue this: "by comparing living primates, including humans, with each other; by discovery and investigation of fossil remains of primates that lived in the past; and by comparing their DNA, proteins, and other molecules" (Ayala, *Am I a Monkey?*, 3).

64. Ayala, *Am I a Monkey?*, 8. Of course, he also draws attention to the fact that this 1 percent is a significant difference. In his textbook, he expounds on the differences, "If one takes into account DNA stretches found in one species but not the other, the two genomes are about 96 percent identical, rather than nearly 99 percent identical as in the case of DNA sequences shared by both species. That is, a large amount of genetic material, about 3 percent or some 90 million DNA nucleotides, have been inserted or deleted since humans and chimps initiated their separate evolutionary ways, about 8–6 Ma" (Conde and Ayala, *Human Evolution*, 49).

not occur, then it would provide a powerful counterargument to the claim that humans and other primates share a common ancestor. When geneticists successfully mapped the human genome, however, they discovered a fusion on human chromosome 2.[65] This provides further confirmation, for Ayala, of common ancestry.

Natural Selection and Teleology

Ayala's case for the *fact of evolution* is persuasive, but his argument concerning how the *fact of evolution* undermines ID is underdeveloped. He does offer two additional critiques of ID, however, which are worthy of careful evaluation. The first is an indirect critique where he defends the notion that natural selection is the primary driving force of evolutionary development. Ayala believes, as mentioned earlier, that this notion was Darwin's greatest discovery. He contends that the fundamental problem with design arguments in biology is that they do not appreciate the creative force of natural selection working on random mutations.[66] As mutations occur within an organism, Ayala explains that selection has the power to increase survivability in those organisms. When this simple process is extended over vast periods of time, then the selection process is capable of incrementally producing large-scale changes.[67] Such changes may often give the appearance of design in certain biological systems, even though this Darwinian mechanism is nonteleological.

---

65. Ayala, *Am I a Monkey?*, 11.

66. Ayala explains, "The conundrum faced by Darwin can hardly be overestimated. The strength of the argument from design to demonstrate the role of the Creator had been forcefully set forth by Paley. Wherever there is function or design, we look for its author. It was Darwin's greatest accomplishment to show that the complex organization and functionality of living beings can be explained as the result of a natural process, natural selection, without any need to resort to a Creator or other external agent.... Darwin went on to provide a natural explanation of design. The seemingly purposeful aspects of living beings could now be explained, like the phenomena of the inanimate world, by the methods of science, as the result of natural laws manifested in natural processes" (Ayala, *Darwin and Intelligent Design*, 19).

67. Conde and Ayala describe the selection process as follows: "The differential reproduction of alternative hereditary variants, determined by the fact that some variants increase the likelihood that the organisms having them will survive and reproduce more successfully than will organisms carrying alternative variants. Selection may occur as a result of differences in survival, in fertility, in rate of development, in mating success, or in any other aspect of the life cycle" (Conde and Ayala, *Human Evolution*, 9).

Of course, Ayala notes that many critics of evolution argue that natural selection is a negative process, and therefore does not have the power to create.[68] Dembski expresses this very critique:

> Natural selection does not so much select for adaptive advantages as rule out maladaptive disadvantages, excluding the latter from survival and reproduction and thus eliminating them from the evolutionary tree. Natural selection is in the business of ruling out possibilities, thereby producing information in the structures and organisms it has retained. An ongoing point of controversy in biology is the extent to which natural selection can generate increases in novel information needed to drive the evolution of life. Some see it as biology's primary source of information. Others see its creative potential in producing information quite limited.[69]

Contra Dembski, Ayala maintains that natural selection is much more than an eliminative process. Instead, natural selection generates real novelty because it "increases the probability of otherwise extremely improbable genetic combinations."[70] *Chance* by itself does not produce improbable genetic combinations, but the combination of *chance* and *necessity* (random mutations and natural selection) increases the creative power of unguided evolution.[71] Elsewhere Ayala explains that "although [natural selection] does not 'create' the component entities upon which it operates (genes and genetic mutations), it does yield 'design,' combinations that could not have existed otherwise and that are beneficial to the organisms."[72] Darwinian

---

68. Ayala, *Darwin and Intelligent Design*, 61–62.
69. Dembski, *Being as Communion*, 20.
70. Ayala, *Darwin and Intelligent Design*, 61–62.
71. Ayala writes, "The theory of evolution conveys chance and necessity intricately conjoined in the stuff of life. Contingency and determinism interlocked in a natural process that has produced the most complex, diverse, and beautiful entities in the universe: the organisms that populate the earth, including humans, who think and love, are endowed with free will and creative powers, and are able to analyze the process of evolution itself that brought them into existence. This was Darwin's fundamental discovery, that there is a process that is creative though not conscious" (Ayala, "From Paley to Darwin," 75).
72. Ayala, *Big Questions*, 33.

evolution, therefore, is not a random process.[73] It is a selective process that has the ability to produce *functional* design within organisms.[74]

So what makes a Darwinian explanation better than a teleological explanation when it comes to functional design within organisms? Ayala contends that natural selection, while giving the *appearance* of design, does not look like a premeditated process. He explains,

> An engineer has a preconception of what he wants to design and will select suitable materials and modify the design so that it fulfills the intended function. On the contrary, natural selection has no foresight, nor does it operate according to some preconceived plan. Rather, it is purely natural process resulting from the interacting properties of physicochemical and biological entities. Natural selection is simply a consequence of the differential

---

73. Ayala notes that mutations are random, but when mutations are selected for a particular advantage, the process of evolution ceases to be random. He writes, "Mutations are said to be accidental, undirected, random, or chance events. These terms are often used as synonyms, but there are at least three different senses in which they are predicated of the mutation process. First, mutations are accidental or chance events, in the sense that they are rare exceptions to the regularity of the process of DNA replication, which normally involves precise copying of the hereditary information, encoded in the nucleotide sequences. Second, mutations are accidental, random, or chance events also because there is no way of knowing whether a given gene or genome will mutate in a particular cell or in a particular generation. We cannot predict which individuals will have a new mutation and which ones will not, nor can we predict which gene will mutate in a given individual. This does not imply that no regularities exist in the mutation process; the regularities are those associated with stochastic processes, to which probabilities can be assigned. There is a definite probability (although it may not have been ascertained) that a given gene will mutate in any given individual. Moreover, it is not true that any mutation is just as likely to occur as any other mutation. Third, mutations are accidental, undirected, random, or chance events in a sense that is very important for evolution: they are unoriented with respect to adaptation. Mutations occur independently of whether or not they are adaptive in the environments where the organisms live. In fact, newly arisen mutations are much more likely to be deleterious than beneficial. It is easy to see why this should be so" (Ayala, "From Paley to Darwin," 73–74). Ayala elsewhere explains, "The combination of genetic units that carries the hereditary information responsible for the formation of the vertebrate eye could have never been produced purely by a random process—not even if we allow for the three and a half billion years during which life has existed on earth. This is the argument advanced by proponents of intelligent design. But evolution is not a process governed by random events" (Ayala, *Darwin and Intelligent Design*, 62).

74. Ayala writes, "As a consequence of natural selection, organisms exhibit design, that is, adaptive organs and functions, but it is not 'intelligent' design, imposed by God as a Supreme Engineer. Rather it is the result of a natural process of selection, promoting the adaptation of organisms to their environments" (Ayala, *Darwin and Intelligent Design*, 13).

survival and reproduction of living beings, as pointed out. It has some appearance of purposefulness because it is conditioned by the environment: which organisms survive and reproduce more effectively depends on which variations they happen to possess that are useful or beneficial to them in the place and at the time where they live.[75]

And since natural design is conditioned by the environment, Ayala suggests that the term *adaptation* is more apt than *design* when speaking about organisms and their features. Gills, for example, were not designed for breathing in water; they were adapted for breathing in water. Legs, similarly, were adapted for walking and wings were adapted for flying.[76] While scientists may refer to such features as *designed*, Ayala clarifies to his readers that scientists are not intending to communicate that such features were actually designed. Rather, they are using design language to express that organisms are adapted to particular environments for survival advantages.

Scientific Problems with Intelligent Design

Developing a proper understanding of natural selection, for Ayala, is foundational for recognizing why design arguments are misguided. Once that understanding is established, he then provides direct responses to specific arguments advanced by ID advocates. Most notable are his critiques of Behe's argument for IC and Dembski's case for SC. In addition to these specific critiques, Ayala also criticizes ID for doing nothing more than reviving Paley's outdated design argument,[77] for being an underhanded political

---

75. Ayala, *Darwin's Gift*, 70.

76. Ayala, *Darwin and Intelligent Design*, 54.

77. Ayala writes, "In the 1990s, several authors, notably biochemist Michael Behe (1996), theorist William Dembski (1995), and law professor Phillip Johnson (2000), among others, revived the argument from design" (Ayala, "Darwin and Intelligent Design," 2:752). Ayala also frequently conflates Paley's argument with the modern ID movement. He further writes, "The argument from design is a two-tined argument. The first prong, as formulated for example by the English author William Paley (1743–1805), asserts that organisms, in their wholes, in their parts, and in their relations to one another and to the environment, appear to have been designed for serving certain functions and to fulfill certain ways of life. The second prong of the argument affirms that only God, an omnipotent and omniscient creator, could account for the diversity, perfection, and functionality of living organisms and their parts" (Ayala, "No Place for Intelligent Design," 365).

ploy to get religion into the science classroom,[78] and for not recognizing MN as an appropriate restriction for scientific investigation.[79] While these additional critiques are worthy of examination, I skip them because they are not pertinent to the overall purpose of this book.[80] For my purposes, it will be enough to assess his critiques of Behe and Dembski.

Ayala spends more time on Behe than Dembski, since he considers Behe "the only proponent of ID who qualifies as a bona fide biologist."[81] Behe's IC argument is an attempt to demonstrate that certain features in biology are incapable of being explained by a Darwinian process. By explicating such features, he wants to test a claim made by Darwin, stating, "If it could be demonstrated that any complex organ existed, which could not possibly have been formed by numerous, successive, slight modifications,

---

78. Ayala contends that authors like Dembski "sought to hide that their argument from design was an argument for the existence of God, so that intelligent design theory could be taught in the public schools, as an alternative to the theory of evolution, without incurring conflict with the United States Constitution, which forbids the endorsement of any religious beliefs in public institutions" (Ayala, *Darwin and Intelligent Design*, 71). Even though ID advocates frequently deny this charge, many ID critics are persuaded that ID advocates are not being genuine. One particular incident that has convinced courts that ID advocates are being disingenuous is the various additions of the ID textbook, *Of Pandas and People*. Early editions used the word "creation" as an alternative to evolution, whereas later editions used the phrase "intelligent design." This has caused many ID critics to suspect that the *real* motivation for ID is to sneak creationism (a religious doctrine) into the biology classroom. Ayala agrees with this critique. He writes, "Explicit reference to God is avoided, so that the 'theory' of ID can be taught in the public schools as an alternative to the theory of evolution without incurring conflict with the U.S. Constitution, which forbids the endorsement of any religious beliefs in public institutions" (Ayala, "No Place for Intelligent Design," 365). While there is some justified concern to Ayala's (and other critics') complaint on this issue, most of it is misguided. Dembski notes that Stoic philosophers from ancient Greece developed a theory of design, which provides one illustration of how one can affirm ID without a committing to a particular religious doctrine of creation. See Dembski, "What Intelligent Design Is Not," 19–20.

79. Ayala explains that if science is the study of the natural world, then our methods of science should strictly involve naturalistic explanations. He writes, "Science has nothing decisive to say about values, whether economic, aesthetic, or moral; about the meaning of life or its purpose; about religious beliefs as such" (Ayala, *Darwin and Intelligent Design*, 100). Ayala further emphasizes that he does not espouse metaphysical naturalism, only methodological naturalism when it comes to scientific investigation. He argues elsewhere, however, "nothing in the world of nature escapes the scientific mode of knowledge, and that we owe this universality to Darwin's revolution" (Ayala, "From Paley to Darwin," 57).

80. For a good critique of Ayala's additional arguments, see Koperski, "Two Bad Ways," 437.

81. Ayala, "No Place for Intelligent Design," 376.

my theory would absolutely break down. But I can find out no such case."[82] Behe, on the other hand, thinks such cases do exist, and cites the bacterial flagellum as one powerful example. He writes,

> As biochemists have begun to examine apparently simple structures like cilia and flagella, they have discovered staggering complexity, with dozens or even hundreds of precisely tailored parts. . . . As the number of required parts increases, the difficulty of gradually putting the system together skyrockets, and the likelihood of indirect scenarios plummets. . . . Darwinian theory has given no explanation for the cilium of flagellum. The overwhelming complexity of the swimming systems push us to think it may never give an explanation.[83]

Darwin could not have imagined, allegedly, the staggering complexity that exists within the most basic units of life. According to Behe, structures like the bacterial flagellum—because of the various interconnect parts—could not possibly have been formed by numerous, successive, slight modifications. Thus Darwin's theory is, at best, incomplete.

Ayala regards Behe's argument as nothing more than a restatement of Paley's idea that "several parts are framed and put together for a purpose."[84] His principled objection to this idea is summarized as follows:

> In different species of bacteria, there are different kinds of flagella, some simpler than the one described by Behe, others just different, even very different, as in the archaea, a very large bacteria-like group of organisms. Moreover, motility in many bacteria is accomplished without flagella at all. Still more, biochemists have shown that some flagellum components may have evolved from secretory systems, which are very similar to the flagellum, but lack some of the flagellum's components (see, for example, Liu & Ochman, 2007; Pallen & Matzke, 2006). The argument for the irreducible complexity of the flagellum is formulated, like other ID arguments, as an *argument from ignorance*: because one author does not know how a complex organ may have come about, it must be the case that it is irreducibly complex. This argument

---

82. Darwin, *Origin of Species*, 142.

83. Behe, *Darwin's Black Box*, 73.

84. Paley, *Natural Theology*, 7. While such an argument worked for Paley's contemporaries, Ayala chides ID advocates for not familiarizing themselves with scientific insights available since the Darwinian revolution. See Ayala, "Darwin and Intelligent Design," 754.

from ignorance dissolves as scientific knowledge advances, or when preexisting scientific knowledge is taken into account.[85]

Put succinctly, IC is simply an argument from ignorance that offers no positive scientific explanation.[86] Ayala continues,

> The claim is that if evolution fails to explain some biological phenomenon, ID must be the correct explanation. This is a misunderstanding of the scientific process. If one explanation fails, it does not necessarily follow that some other proposed explanation is correct. Explanations must stand on their own evidence, not on the failure of their alternatives. Scientific explanations or hypotheses are creations of the mind, conjectures, imaginative exploits about the makeup and operation of the natural world. It is the imaginative preconception of what might be true in a particular case that guides observations and experiments designed to test whether a hypothesis is correct.[87]

These paragraphs reference two related but distinct complaints with ID. First, ID is structured as a negative argument against Darwinian mechanisms, rather than a positive argument for design. Ayala contends that ID does not offer a proposition to test, "but makes only the lame claim that the theory of evolution by natural selection cannot account for the complexity of organisms."[88] As such, ID is ostensibly an argument based upon scientific ignorance. This relates to Ayala's second complaint, namely, that scientific explanations ought to offer evidence, rather than merely critiquing already existing theories. Highlighting the shortcomings in evolutionary theory, according to Ayala, does nothing to establish

---

85. Ayala, "No Place for Intelligent Design," 374.

86. Ayala further writes, "the ID 'explanation' is not a scientific hypothesis that can be tested by observation and experiment. Indeed, ID does not advance any explanation, but it amounts only to a negative claim: that the relevant evolutionary explanations are not satisfactory" (ibid., 374). Ayala goes on further to describe Behe's shortcomings, not only in terms of methodology, but also in terms of his scientific ignorance. In reference to the mechanisms regarding blood clotting, Behe claimed in 1996 that "*no one on earth has the vaguest idea how the coagulation cascade came to be*" (Behe, *Darwin's Black Box*, 97). Ayala is astonished by Behe's claim and responds, "[There are] numerous scientific papers about the evolution of the various components of the blood-clotting mechanisms in vertebrates, including 'The Evolution of Vertebrate Blood Coagulation: A case of Yin and Yang' by the eminent biochemist Russell F. Doolittle, published in 1993" (Ayala, "No Place for Intelligent Design," 377).

87. Ayala, "No Place for Intelligent Design," 375.

88. Ayala, "No Place for Intelligent Design," 376.

a case for ID. ID is a separate idea, which needs positive evidence to gain respect within the scientific community.

In addition to these principled objections against IC, Ayala claims that biochemists have already shown that the bacterial flagellum is not irreducibly complex, and that there are plausible Darwinian accounts demonstrating how complex systems like the bacterial flagellum can arise through gradual and cumulative evolutionary processes.[89] He notes, as an example, the type-III secretory system (TTSS)—stating that it essentially the same structure as Behe's flagellum, although lacking the motor protein.[90]

Proponents of ID, however, have been long familiar with TTSS, and they claim that it is not an evolutionary precursor to the flagellum. Dembski and Wells, for example, cite an article in the *Journal of Molecular Microbiology and Biotechnology* (published in 2000) to demonstrate that TTSS evolved from the bacterial flagellum, rather than the other way around.[91] They argue,

> At best, the bacterial flagellum could explain the evolution of the TTSS. But even that isn't quite right. The TTSS is, after all, much simpler than the flagellum. The flagellum requires an additional thirty or forty proteins, which in turn need to be accounted for. Evolution needs to explain the emergence of complexity from simplicity. But if the TTSS (de-)evolved from the flagellum, then we've done the exact opposite (i.e., we've explained the simpler in terms of the more complex).[92]

Dembski and Wells further restate that the scientific literature shows "a complete absence of detailed, testable, step-by-step proposals for how coevolution and co-option could actually produce irreducibly complex biochemical systems."[93] Whether Dembski and Wells correctly interpret this literature is a question beyond the scope of this book. Ayala's objections to the idea that design can be detected in biology, however, are germane for my purposes, and Behe's IC is one way that ID theorists have articulated

---

89. Ayala, *Darwin and Intelligent Design*, 14. Later Ayala explains that "evolutionists have pointed out, again and again, with supporting evidence, that organs and other components of living beings are not irreducibly complex—they do not come about suddenly, or in one fell swoop" (Ayala, *Darwin and Intelligent Design*, 78).
90. Ayala, *Darwin and Intelligent Design*, 81.
91. L. Nguyen, et al., "Phylogenetic Analyses," 125–44.
92. Dembski and Wells, *Design of Life*, 155.
93. Dembski and Wells, *Design of Life*, 155.

a method for detecting design. Unfortunately, Ayala's critique of IC is not aimed at critiquing the method itself; rather it simply contends that Behe's proposed examples fall short of being irreducibly complex.

This is not to say, of course, that Ayala is entirely silent on the idea of design detection. When considering Dembski's method of SC, he does focus his critique on the method itself. But again, Ayala's critique unfortunately falls short—this time because it is brief, oversimplified, and awfully close to misrepresenting Dembski's case for SC. Ayala explains Dembski's contribution to ID as follows:

> The mathematically trained William Dembski, (1995, 2002) is another ID proponent who has used supposedly scientific arguments to demonstrate the irreducible complexity of organisms. According to Dembski, organisms exhibit "complex specified information," which is information that has a very low prior probability and, therefore, high information content. Dembski argues that mutation and natural selection are incapable of generating such highly improbable states of affairs.[94]

Recognizing the mathematical contributions of Dembski, Ayala refers to an equation where Dembski calculates that chances of a flagellum coming into existence as 10^{-1170}. While such a number undoubtedly seems staggering, Ayala asserts that it is actually irrelevant since "Dembski does not take into account the role of natural selection and makes a number of erroneous assumptions."[95] But Ayala's claim that Dembski does not account for natural selection is peculiar. In the very paragraph that Ayala cites, he shows that Dembski wrote "mutation *and natural selection* are incapable of generating highly improbable states of affairs." Why then would Ayala assume that Dembski does not take into account the role of natural selection? Ayala seems to gloss over Dembski's actual words, but what is more troubling is that Dembski provides extensive arguments regarding the inadequacy of natural selection to generate SC.[96] Ayala never mentions those arguments, and therefore at best he overstates his critique of Dembski, and at worst he is unaware of Dembski's work on natural selection.

Ayala continues his critique of Dembski by claiming that other authors have pointed out numerous erroneous assumptions within his

---

94. Ayala, "No Place for Intelligent Design," 378.
95. Ayala, "No Place for Intelligent Design," 378.
96. I examine those arguments in chapter 4.

equations.[97] After referencing a few articles that critique Dembski's argument, he maintains that Dembski's numerological exercises suffer from several fatal flaws. Regrettably, Ayala only mentions one apparent flaw.[98] He cites Scott F. Gilbert and the Swarthmore College Evolution and Developmental Seminar, who argue,

> Some of the Intelligent Design's more powerful arguments depend on a simple fallacy: the assumption of an end point.... [ID proponents claims that] it is impossible to evolve a particular protein because it has 100 amino acids and the chance of this occurring randomly is 1 in 20^{100}.... But such supporters of ID don't know a billionth of how impossible it is! Let's say that your mother ovulated 500 eggs during her life and that your father produced 2 X 10^{12} sperm. The chances of *you* being born, then, are 1 in 10^{15} ... [and] the chances of your grandparents giving rise to you is 1 in 10^{45}. Another reason not to argument with the Intelligent Design people, then, is that, by their own logic, they cannot exist.[99]

The apparent flaw mentioned above is that Dembski mistakenly assumes a predetermined end into his equation. When one makes such an assumption, then everything seems improbable, including the chances of me being the offspring of my grandparents. Ayala emphasizes that improbable events happen all the time, and that Dembski's main problem is that he reasons backwards.[100] A close reading of Dembski's *The Design Inference*, however, shows that Dembski does not make this mistake. I will attempt to demonstrate this in chapter 4, where I articulate Dembski's method for detecting design.

After examining Ayala's scientific case against ID, I maintain that he provides only two relevant critiques of ID. Those critiques include his case that random mutations working on natural selection are the sole mechanisms driving evolutionary development, and his contention that Dembski's equations for SC begin with the end in mind. In chapter 4, I show that both of those critiques are wrongheaded. In the next chapter, however, I turn to Ayala's theological critique of ID, which centers on the problem of dysteleology.

---

97. He refers readers specifically to papers in Dembski and Ruse, *Debating Design*; Pennock, *Intelligent Design Creationism*. He also refers to Perakh, *Unintelligent Design*; "There Is a Free Lunch after All," 153–71; Wolpert, "William Dembski's Treatment," 12; Felsenstein, "Has Natural Selection Been Refuted?," 21–26.

98. Ayala, "No Place for Intelligent Design," 378.

99. Gilbert, et al., "Aerodynamics of Flying Carpets," 44–45.

100. Ayala, *Darwin and Intelligent Design*, 84.

3

A Theological Critique of Design in Biology

THIS CHAPTER DEVELOPS THE central philosophical problem of this book, namely, the assertion that suboptimal design in biology undermines the ID project. I call this a philosophical problem, rather than a theological problem, because my primary concern is to assess whether design is an appropriate mode of causation in biology. As such, I am not interested in developing a theodicy, nor am I interested in speculating on the nature or potential motives of the designing agent.

To be clear, however, Ayala's dysteleological argument is presented as a theological critique against ID. For this reason, I cannot completely avoid the theological dimensions of his argument. Specifically, Ayala maintains that divine design is inconsistent with divine goodness, because scientists have discovered numerous imperfections in biology.[1] He further argues that the central premise of ID is that functional design provides evidence for an intelligent designer, and then challenges this premise—stating that if functional design provides evidence for an all-wise Creator, then dysfunctional design should provide evidence for an unintelligent Creator.[2]

---

1. Ayala writes, "The theory of intelligent design is not good theology either, because it leads to conclusions about the nature of the designer quite different from those of omniscience, omnipotence, and benevolence that Christian theology predicates of God" (Ayala, *Darwin and Intelligent Design*, 86). Elsewhere, Ayala writes, "This point depends on a particular view of God—shared by many people of faith—as omniscient, omnipotent, and benevolent. This point also depends on our knowledge of the natural world and, particularly, of the living world. The natural world abounds in catastrophes, disasters, imperfections, dysfunctions, suffering, and cruelty" (Ayala, "Charles Darwin," 21).

2. In chapter 4, I will show that this definition of ID is simplistic and misguided. To support his claim, however, Ayala refers to Paley's argument stating that the human eye provides "conclusive evidence of an all-wise Creator" (Ayala, "Chance and Necessity," 233).

Religious believers, therefore, should find comfort in the fact that Darwin overturned the design argument.[3]

Ayala's theological argument against ID could be classified as a subset of the traditional problem of evil. In fact, he introduces his argument by referring to David Hume's famous articulation of the problem: "Is [God] willing to prevent evil, but not able? Then he is impotent. Is he able, but not willing? Then he is malevolent. Is he both able and willing? Whence then evil?"[4] Ayala applies Hume's argument to natural evil and, more specifically, to biological dysfunctions, cruelties, and oddities. He emphasizes that modern biology enhances the problem of natural evil because it reveals countless examples of imperfect design within living systems. If one claims that God is responsible for the intricate design of life, then, Ayala responds that such a claim leads logically to the notion that God is also responsible for the imperfections of life.[5]

Before Darwin, Ayala claims that traditional Christian theology did not have a respectable theodicy for natural evil.[6] It had solutions to the problem of moral evil, and, for Ayala, the best solution has always been the free-will defense. According to this defense, God is not morally responsible for the free acts of human agents. Thus, when a brutal dictator like Mao Zedong

3. Ayala explains, "I assert that scientific knowledge, the theory of evolution in particular, is consistent with religious belief in God, whereas creationism and intelligent design are not. This point depends on a particular view of God—shared by many people of faith—as omniscient, omnipotent, and benevolent. This point also depends on our knowledge of the natural world and, particularly, of the living world" (Ayala, "Charles Darwin," 21).

4. Ayala, "Darwin and Intelligent Design," 763. Of course, this idea is not original to Hume. Epicurus asked the same question: "God either wants to eliminate bad things and cannot, or can but does not want to, or neither wishes to nor can, or both wants to and can. If he wants to and cannot, he is weak—and this does not apply to god. If he wants to and can, which is the only thing fitting for a god, where then to bad things come from? Or why does he not eliminate them?" See Inwood and Gerson, *Epicurus Reader*, 97.

5. Ayala, *Am I a Monkey?*, 77. Some might argue that examples of imperfections are rare. While Ayala disagrees with this claim, he concedes and responds, "Even if the dysfunctions, cruelties, and sadism of the living world were rare, which they are not, they would still need to be attributed to the Designer if the Designer had designed the living world" (Ayala, *Darwin and Intelligent Design*, 9).

6. Ayala, *Darwin's Gift*, 4. Contra Ayala, Alvin Plantinga argues that philosophers and theologians addressed the problem of natural evil well before Darwin. He explains, "it didn't take Darwin to enable us to see that nature, in Tennyson's phrase (which antedates the publication of *the Origin of Species* by more than a decade), is 'red in tooth and claw'; nor does it take Darwin to enable us to see that the earth is old, and that during much of its history animals have suffered" (Plantinga, *Where the Conflict Really Lies*, 56–57).

developed severe political policies that resulted in the deaths of 70 million people, God was not to blame. Mao was to blame.

Ayala contends that Darwin's theory of evolution provides a similar justification for theologians hoping to solve the problem of natural evil. Darwin's innovative ideas introduce a *natural free-will defense* for the various imperfections within the world of biology, because Darwinian evolution asserts that natural selection and random mutations are the sole driving forces of all biological development. Thus, when life displays examples of imperfection within biological systems, God is not to blame. The processes of natural selection and random mutation are to blame. For this reason, Ayala contends,

> People of faith would do well to acknowledge Darwin's revolution and accept natural selection as the process that accounts for the design of organisms, as well as for the dysfunctions, oddities, and cruelties that pervade the world of life. Evolution makes it possible to attribute these mishaps to the natural processes (which have no moral implications) rather than to the direct creation of specific design of the Creator.[7]

While Darwin is often regarded as an enemy of religion, Ayala insists that he is actually a friend.[8] To further articulate Ayala's argument, I offer the following formulation, which was introduced in chapter 1:[9]

1. A God who is omniscient, omnipotent, and benevolent would not create organisms with suboptimal design (assumption).

2. There are organisms that display features of suboptimal design in biology (as suggested by modern science).

3. ID states that functional organisms were created by God (Ayala's definition of ID).

---

7. Ayala, *Am I a Monkey?*, 78.

8. Ayala writes, "As Aubrey Moore put it in 1891, 'Darwinism appeared, and, under the guise of a foe, did the work of a friend.' The theory of evolution, which at first had seemed to remove the need for God in the world, now has convincingly removed the need to explain the world's imperfections as failed outcomes of God's design" (Ayala, "Darwin and Intelligent Design," 763).

9. While I think this formulation accurately represents Ayala's theological case against ID, Ayala never formulates his argument. This is my best attempt to represent his theological case against ID.

4. If functional organisms were created by God, then one should also assume that organisms displaying features of suboptimal design were also created by God (Ayala's assumed implication of 3).
5. ID assumes that God created organisms that display features of suboptimal design (3 and 4).
6. ID is inconsistent with a God who is omniscient, omnipotent, and benevolent (1 and 5).
7. On the other hand, the theory of evolution states that *all organisms* originated through purely natural processes (Ayala's definition of evolution).
8. If all organisms originated through purely natural processes, then organisms that display features of suboptimal design also originated through purely natural processes (the logical implication of 7).
9. To state that organisms originated through purely natural processes implies that God did not create those organisms (clarification of 7 and 8).
10. The theory of evolution states that God did not create organisms that display features of suboptimal design (7, 8, and 9).
11. The theory of evolution is consistent with a God who is omniscient, omnipotent, and benevolent (1 and 10).
12. ∴ An omniscient, omnipotent, and omnibenevolent God is more consistent with evolution than with ID (6 and 11).

While I am not convinced that my articulation of Ayala's argument is sound, I do think it clarifies and provides an outline of Ayala's theological objections to ID.

God and Suboptimal Design

The central assumption in Ayala's argument is that a God who is omniscient, omnipotent, and benevolent would not create organisms with suboptimal design (Premise 1). He further believes that those who deny this assumption are committing blasphemy.[10] Ayala explains, "The defective design of organisms could be attributed to the gods of the ancient Greeks, Romans, and Egyptians, who fought with one another, made blunders, and

10. Ayala, *Darwin's Gift*, 160.

were clumsy in their endeavors. But, in my view, it is not compatible with special action by the omniscient and omnipotent God of Judaism, Christianity, and Islam."[11] This passage is revealing because it shows that Ayala's dysteleological argument is not really a critique of ID. That is, he is not arguing that the evidence of defective design in biology negates the notion of actual design. He instead argues that imperfect design negates the notion of a creator with traditional omni-attributes. Strictly speaking, then, Ayala's argument is directed only at people with specific religious beliefs, making it irrelevant to the central claims of ID.

Moreover, Ayala's problem is not new for Christian theologians. There is a long tradition of Christian theologians attempting to reconcile the omni-attributes with the presence of suboptimal design. One should recognize, therefore, that Ayala's theodicy is simply one attempt to solve this problem, and the heart of his attempt focuses on the notion that God was not *directly* responsible for suboptimal design.[12] In other words, he argues that God did not create vestigial organs *ex nihilo*; rather, he created the process of evolution, which in turn created vestigial organs. Of course this still implies that God created vestigial organs, but he did so *indirectly*. For Ayala's first premise to carry weight as a theological objection, he needs to defend the notion that an *indirect* creation of suboptimal design makes God less responsible than a *direct* creation of suboptimal design. If Ayala cannot substantiate this claim, then the rest of his argument rests on a faulty assumption.

Suboptimal Design in Biology

I consider Ayala's second premise well established given the examples he cites.[13] He begins with the simple fact that 99 percent of all species that ever

---

11. Ayala, "From Paley to Darwin," 66.

12. Ayala writes, "[Think about] badly designed human jaws, parasites that kill millions of children, and poorly designed human reproductive system that accounts for millions of miscarriages every year in the world. If these dreadful happenings come about by *direct design* by God, God would seem responsible for the consequences. If engineers design cars that explode when you turn on the ignition key, they are accountable. But if the dreadful happenings come about by natural processes (evolution), there are no moral implications, because natural processes do not entail moral values" (Ayala, "Darwin and Intelligent Design," 765, emphasis added).

13. Of course, one could argue that Ayala's interpretations of these examples are subjective. What makes the process of evolution a wasteful process? Why should one

lived on the earth have become extinct. This fact, for Ayala, demonstrates that the evolutionary process for creating life has been a wasteful, rather than efficient, process. If evolution were a teleological process, however, one would presumably expect that far less than 1 billion species would have gone extinct.[14] Ayala asserts that the God of Christianity would not intentionally plan mass extinctions, suffering in the animal kingdom, and a survival-of-the-fittest environment as the means of achieving his ultimate goals and purposes. This theological complaint is not an argument against the evolutionary process; rather it is an argument against incorporating teleology into the evolutionary process. In other words, the wasteful processes of evolutionary development are not a theological problem for Ayala because he regards those processes as blind and unguided.

In addition to the general wastefulness of evolution, Ayala mentions current examples of imperfect design, such as the suboptimal design of the human eye. Those familiar with the history of teleological arguments will notice the rhetorical force of citing the human eye as an example of suboptimal design, given that many design advocates view the eye as a prime example of design. Ayala, however, emphasizes the abnormal aspects of the human eye. For example, the path that light needs to travel to reach the cones and rods in the retina is less than optimal. To achieve vision, light must pass through the pupil, to the back of the eye, through the retina, and eventually to the photoreceptors—the cones and rods that convert light into electrical signals at the back of the retina. Once light hits the retina, it travels through a series of ganglion and bipolar cells before reaching the cones and rods. At this point, the light produces chemical changes within the cones and rods, and then sends electrical signals back through the bipolar and ganglion cells and eventually culminates in the optic nerve. This path is counterintuitive from an engineering perspective. Ayala argues that an intelligent designer would make the retina more efficient by placing the photoreceptors in front of the bipolar and ganglion

---

concede that the human eye contains an example of suboptimal design? I agree that there is an element of subjectivity in answering such questions, however, it is the same subjectivity allowed for ID advocates. If one accepts the principled arguments for ID, therefore, it seems that one can also accept the principled arguments for suboptimal design.

14. Ayala, "From Paley to Darwin," 72. Elsewhere, he writes, "We know that more than 99 percent of all species that have ever lived on Earth have become extinct without issue. Thus, since the beginning of life on Earth 3.5 billion years ago, the number of different species that have lived on our planet is likely to be more than 1 billion" (Ayala, *Darwin's Gift*, 71).

cells. If the human eye is designed, therefore, it follows that the human eye is not *intelligently* designed.

To make matters worse, the backwards wiring of the retina is not the only problem with the human eye. Ayala notes that there are no photoreceptors on the optic disk, which accounts for a blind spot that exists within our visual field. He further reports that such a blind spot is not universal within the animal kingdom:

> The most advanced mollusk eye is found in the octopus and the squid. It is just as complex and effective as the human eye and lacks the blind spot. The imperfection of the blind spot in the human eye is due to the fact that the nerve fibers of the human eye are collected inside the eye cavity, so that the optic nerve has to cross the retina on its way to the brain.[15]

After skillfully highlighting the shortcomings of the human eye compared to the most advance mollusk eye, Ayala rhetorically asks, "Did the Creator have greater love for squids than for humans and thus exhibit greater care in designing their eyes than ours?"[16] Questions like this underscore Ayala's main theological objection to ID.

Ayala additionally cites the small size of the human jaw (which makes it necessary to remove wisdom teeth for many adults), and the narrow size of the human birth canal (which results in thousands upon thousands of babies and mothers dying during delivery).[17] He highlights the strange fact that human arms and legs have the same arrangement of bones, muscles, and nerves as many other mammals that use those arrangements for entirely different functions—implying that these arrangements are not optimally designed for every function in every mammal.[18] Ayala then concludes by listing numerous instances of cruelty in nature, including

> the actions of predators (say, a chimpanzee) tearing apart their prey (say, a small monkey held alive and screaming by a

---

15. Ayala, *Darwin and Intelligent Design*, 67.

16. Ayala, *Am I a Monkey?*, 77.

17. Ayala notes that "20 percent of all recognized human pregnancies end in spontaneous miscarriage during the first two months of pregnancy" (Ayala, *Darwin's Gift*, 157).

18. For example, bats use the arrangement of bones in their arms and hands for flying, rather than typing on a computer. Objects that are designed by engineers do not display such similarities. Ayala explains, "An engineer who would design cars and airplanes, or wings and wheels, using the same material arranged in a similar pattern, would surely be fired" (Ayala, *Darwin's Gift*, 156).

chimpanzee biting large flesh morsels from it) or parasites destroying the functional organs of their hosts but also, and very abundantly, interactions between organisms of the same species, including between mates. A well-known example is the female praying mantis, which devours the male after coitus is completed. Less familiar is the fact that, if she gets the opportunity, the female will eat the head of the male *before* mating; thrashing the headless male mantis into spasms of "sexual frenzy" allows the female to connect his genitalia with hers.[19]

When taken together, these various examples build a compelling case that dysfunctions, imperfections, and cruelties do exist in nature.[20]

Intelligent Versus Suboptimal Design

How, then, should one understand these various dysfunctions, imperfections, and cruelties? The key claim in Ayala's argument is that Darwinian evolution gets God off the hook for suboptimal design, thus providing warrant for the additional claim that ID is inconsistent with traditional theistic belief. Nature, and specifically the processes of evolutionary biology, must be completely free of design from Ayala's perspective. He cites American philosopher David Hull to explain why:

> What kind of God can one infer from the sort of phenomena epitomized by the species on Darwin's Galapagos Islands? The evolutionary process is rife with happenstance, contingency, incredible waste, death, pain and horror. . . . Whatever the God implied by evolutionary theory and the data of natural selection may be like, he is not the Protestant God of waste not, want not.

---

19. Ayala, *Darwin and Intelligent Design*, 88. Ayala further explains, "We know that some deficiencies are not just imperfections, but they are outright dysfunctional, jeopardizing the very function the organ or part is supposed to serve. Moreover, carnivorous predators behave in ways that by human standards would be judged cruel, and parasites seem designed with a sadistic purpose, since they exist by harming other organisms. The mating interactions between male and female in some insects, spiders, and other organisms would also be judged cruel and even sadistic by human standards" (Ayala, *Darwin and Intelligent Design*, 8).

20. To consider a few more examples, Ayala mentions Tsunamis bringing destruction and death; the volcanic eruptions that erased Pompeii and Herculaneum, floods and droughts, lions that devour their prey, malaria, and parasites that kill millions of humans every year and make 500 million sick. See Ayala, "Charles Darwin," 21. Similarly, Robert John Russell refers to natural evil as "disease, suffering, death of individual organisms and the extinction of species" (Russell, "Is Evil Evolving?," 309).

> He is also not the loving God who cares about his productions. He is not even the awful God pictured in the Book of Job. The God of the Galapagos is careless, wasteful, indifferent, almost diabolical. He is certainly not the sort of God whom anyone would be inclined to pray.[21]

Ironically, Ayala does not see Hull's criticism as a problem for theologians who embrace Darwinian evolution. He views this exclusively as an argument against ID. Why? Because, according to Ayala, ID argues that functional structures within organisms provide evidence that God created those structures (Premise 3). But if God intentionally designed such structures, then he also intentionally designed the evolutionary process that brought those structures into existence. And if functional design provides evidence for *intelligent* design, then the appearance of cruelty and dysfunction within the evolutionary process should provide evidence for *unintelligent* design (Premise 4). ID, then, implies that God's creation is suboptimally designed, which is inconsistent with a God who is omniscient, omnipotent, and benevolent (Premises 5 and 6). This is why Ayala writes that "ID is bad religion, bad theology, because it implies that the designer has undesirable attributes that we don't want to predicate about God."[22]

Ayala then considers how ID advocates might respond to the problems he expresses above. Specifically, he considers Paley's and Behe's responses to the problem of suboptimal design. He cites Paley as arguing, "Irregularities and imperfections are of little or no weight . . . but they are to be taken in conjunction with the unexceptionable evidences which we possess of skill, power, and benevolence displayed in other instances."[23] This response is unpersuasive to Ayala, because, to restate his central argument, "If functional design manifests an intelligent designer, why should not deficiencies indicate that the designer is less than omniscient, or less than omnipotent, or less than omnificent?"[24] Ayala thus maintains that Paley is inconsistent, and, furthermore, stresses the point that Paley does not provide appropriate details regarding the nature of dysfunctions within the natural world.

The problem with Ayala's perspective, however, is that he leaves out an important passage that better explains Paley's position. Paley's counterargument does not depend upon specific details regarding cruelties that exist

21. Hull, "God of the Galapagos," 485–86.
22. Ayala, *Darwin's Gift*, 12.
23. Paley, *Natural Theology*, 8.
24. Ayala, *Darwin and Intelligent Design*, 8.

within the animal kingdom. He is making a principled argument that imperfections do not negate design. This is seen clearly when one looks at the difference between warts and eyes. Both are parts of the human body, but Paley does not argue that both are designed. Some features display design, and others do not. Paley explains his idea at length:

> When we are enquiring simply after the *existence* of an intelligent Creator, imperfection, inaccuracy, liability to disorder, occasional irregularities, may subsist, in a considerable degree, without inducing any doubt into the question: just as a watch may frequently go wrong, seldom perhaps exactly right, may be faulty in some parts, defective in some, without the smallest ground of suspicion from thence arising, that it was not a watch; not made; or not made for the purpose ascribed to it. When faults are pointed out, and when a question is started concerning the skill of the artist, or the dexterity with which the work is executed, then indeed, in order to defend these qualities from accusation, we must be able, either to expose some intractableness and imperfection in the materials, or point out some invincible difficulty in the execution, into which imperfection and difficulty the matter of complaint may be resolved; or, if we cannot do this, we must adduce such specimens of consummate art and contrivance proceeding from the same hand, as may convince the enquirer, of the existence, in the case before him, of impediments like those which we have mentioned, although, what from the nature of the case is very likely to happen, they be unknown and unperceived by him. This we must do in order to vindicate the artist's skill, or, at least, the perfection of it; as we must also judge of his intention, and of the provisions employed in fulfilling that intention, not from an instance in which they fail, but from the great plurality of instances in which they succeed. But, after all, these are different questions from the question of the artist's existence; or, not: and the questions ought always to be kept separate in the mind.[25]

A careful reading of this paragraph should undermine Ayala's dysteleological critique of Paley, since Paley's foundational question is whether life provides evidence for an intelligent Creator.[26] To mention instances of imperfect design, therefore, is to miss Paley's point. Paley is not arguing that

25. Paley, *Natural Theology*, 35.
26. The word "intelligent" refers generally to a conscious creator. Paley certainly believes that the God of the Bible is responsible for the design of life, but here he is not arguing for specific attributes within the creator—such as being omnipresent, omnipotent, etc.

everything in biology is designed, nor is he contending that any instance of design is optimal. His only claim is that *some features* of the living world really are designed. This claim could certainly be wrong, but a close reading of Paley shows that Ayala is incorrect to assert that Paley's argument is inconsistent with examples of suboptimal design.

Likewise, Ayala's appraisal of Behe's response to suboptimal design is equally problematic. He quotes Behe's response to imperfections as follows:

> The argument from imperfection overlooks the possibility that the designer might have multiple motives, with engineering excellence oftentimes relegated to a secondary role.... The reasons that a designer would or would not do anything are vitally impossible to know unless the designer tells you specifically what those reasons are.[27]

After providing this passage, Ayala asserts that Behe's statement "might have theological validity, but it destroys intelligent design as a scientific hypothesis, because it provides it with an empirically impenetrable shield against predictions of how 'intelligent' or 'perfect' a design will be."[28]

The problem with Ayala's response to Behe should be clear. Ayala claims that Behe is removing ID from science by making it impossible to predict how intelligent or perfect the design will be. For Ayala, this move might be permissible theologically, but not scientifically. That is exactly Behe's point, however. Questions about theodicy are not relevant to science. Behe expounds on this point in *The Edge of Evolution*:

> Whether on balance one thinks life was a worthwhile project or not—whether the designer of life was a dope, a demon, or a deity—that's a topic on which opinions over the millennia have differed considerably. Each argument has some merit.... Maybe the designer *isn't* all that beneficent or omnipotent. Science can't answer questions like that.[29]

If Behe's theological response to the problem of dysteleology makes ID unscientific, then Ayala's theological response to the same problem should equally make Darwinism unscientific. J.P. Moreland makes a similar point when he writes,

---

27. Behe, *Darwin's Black Box*, 223. Also cited in Ayala, *Darwin and Intelligent Design*, 85.

28. Ayala, *Darwin and Intelligent Design*, 85–86.

29. Behe, *Edge of Evolution*, 238–39.

> Cases of alleged "bad or inefficient design" are used by scientists to argue that these cases falsify the notion of a god, because if such a god existed, surely he could do a better job than he did in the bad, inefficient cases. Well, if a theological model of God can be used to *falsify* that model, why can't a different theological model be used to provide scientific *evidence* for that model? Advocates of methodological naturalism can't have it both ways. On the one hand, they claim that *science must adopt methodological naturalism and that theological propositions are entirely outside the range of science.* On the other hand, for more than 150 years scientists have used *theological models of an incompetent, inept designer to test against the evidence of biology and paleontology to show that the evidence demonstrates that a designer does not exist.* This sounds like a "reverse intelligent design" to me.[30]

While Moreland is specifically addressing atheists who reject ID, his argument also applies to Ayala. Specifically, Ayala seems to suggest that certain theological positions are scientific—presumably positions where God does not provide evidence of design within creation—whereas others—particularly those offered by ID advocates—are unscientific. He cannot have it both ways. If suboptimal design provides evidence for his theological model, then instances of intricate design should provide evidence for a theological model consistent with ID.

Natural Selection and Suboptimal Design

While Ayala's responses to Paley and Behe are unpersuasive, there remains an important question regarding the theological merits of his critique. Perhaps general design is consistent with the known imperfections in biology. This does not mean that the design of a God with omni-attributes is consistent with the known imperfections in biology. To appreciate the force of Ayala's theological critique against ID, one needs to understand his solution to the problem of natural evil. Ayala maintains that the theory of evolution demonstrates that *all organisms* originated through a purely natural process—natural selection operating on random mutations (Premise 7).[31] This idea has implications for theodicy, because if all organisms originated through purely natural processes, then organisms that display features of suboptimal design also originated through

---

30. Moreland, *Scientism and Secularism*, 167–68.
31. In chapter 2, I clarified that Ayala calls this the *mechanism of evolution*.

purely natural processes (Premise 8). It follows, then, that suboptimal design is consistent with the character of God, since God is not the direct originator of suboptimal design. Suboptimal design is simply the result of natural processes that cannot be held to moral standards.[32] Darwin's discovery of natural selection, therefore, was a gift to science and religion because it demonstrated that God is not responsible for suboptimal design (Premises 9 and 10). Thus, evolution is consistent with a God who is omniscient, omnipotent, and benevolent (Premise 11).

Ayala's evolutionary theodicy might seem feasible on the surface, but there are deeper problems that deserve attention. Robert John Russell, for example, highlights a significant difficulty with all evolutionary theodicies when he asks, "If, according to theistic evolution, God acts to create life through evolution, and since evolution necessarily includes disease, suffering, death and extinction, does this make God responsible for natural evil and, in turn render faith in God unintelligible?[33] This question, as explained by Chris Doran, raises a significant challenge for Ayala's theodicy. Doran writes,

> Ayala suggests that Christians are home free now that the "bad" design we see in the universe can be "blamed on/attributed to" evolutionary processes rather than God. It seems to me that the question that Ayala avoids is the question that still must be asked: Who created the laws that govern evolutionary processes? If we pursue this avenue of thought, then the issue is not whether the design of the universe or particular features in our universe are bad, imperfect, or cruel, but rather whether God imbuing the universe with the freedom to "create" itself through evolutionary processes is really worth it. . . . It's easy to take science seriously and say that God creates through evolutionary processes. It's quite another thing to swallow the fact that God then creates through pain, predation, and extinction.[34]

Doran's critique is convincing, although he wrongly asserts that Ayala avoids his question. Instead, Ayala's brief answer is that there is a correlation between God giving humanity free will and God giving the natural world the capacity to create.[35] A world without human freedom, according

32. Ayala, *Am I a Monkey?*, 80.
33. Russell, "Is Evil Evolving?," 309.
34. Doran, "From Atheism to Theodicy," 340.
35. One could also argue that the creation story in *Genesis* supports the idea that the natural world has the capacity to create. Ernan McMullin writes, "Theologians of

to Ayala, is less ideal than a world with freedom.[36] Similarly, a world that is meticulously controlled world, resulting in no natural suffering or defects, is less ideal than a free world. He explains,

> Before modern physical science came about, God (in some religious views) caused rain, drought, volcanic eruptions, and the like, to reward or punish people. This view entails that God would have caused the tsunami that killed 200,000 Indonesians a few years ago. That would seem incompatible with a benevolent God. However, we now know that tsunamis and other "natural" catastrophes come about by natural processes. Natural processes don't entail moral values. Some critics might say, "that does not excuse God, because God created the world as it is. God could have created a different world, without catastrophes." Yes, according to some belief systems, God could have created a different world. But that would not be a creative universe, where galaxies form, stars and planetary systems come about, and continents drift causing earthquakes. The world that we have is creative and more exciting than a static world. This argument will not convince all, but is a valid argument for some as an account of physical evil, and many theologians use it, whether implicitly or explicitly.[37]

---

the early Church were struck by the way in which the first verses of *Genesis* describe the origins of living things; God said: 'Let the earth bring forth nourishing crops . . . and fruit trees bearing fruit'; 'Let the waters bring forth living creatures and birds to fly above the earth'; 'Let the earth bring forth living creatures according to their kinds: cattle, creeping things, and beasts of the earth.' It seemed as though the Creator had, in the work of the Six Days, conferred successively upon waters and earth the power to bring forth all the living kinds" (McMullin, "Darwin and the Other Christian Tradition," 292).

36. Ayala writes, "Critics might say that [free will] does not excuse God, because God could have created humans without free will (whatever these 'humans' may have been called and been like). But one could reasonably argue that 'humans' without free will would be a very different kind of creature, a being much less interesting and creative than humans are. Robots are not a good replacement for humans; robots do not perform virtuous deeds" (Ayala, "Evolution Beyond Biology," 383).

37. Ayala, "Darwin and Intelligent Design," 764–65. Of course, to embrace this argument, one must find the free will defense for moral evil plausible, which would presumable involve constructing a molinist, open theist, or panentheist theology. My best educated guess is that Ayala aligns most closely with panentheism. I say this because he quotes favorably Arthur Peacocke: "Any static conception of the way in which God sustains and holds the cosmos in being is therefore precluded, for new entities, structures, and processes appear in the course of time, so that God's action as Creator is both past and present: it is continuous. . . . The traditional notion of God *sustaining* the world in its general order and structure now has to be enriched by a dynamic and creative dimension" (Ayala, "Charles Darwin," 20).

Put succinctly, Ayala argues that a world of life with evolution is much more exciting than a world without it.[38]

This *more exciting world* theodicy seems, according to theologians like Oliver Puts, incomplete and vague.[39] For whom is this creation exciting? Is it more exciting for the predator or for the prey? When pushed for clarity on such questions, Ayala responds, "I am writing as a scientist concerned about the theological implications of science. Thus, I have repeatedly asserted, using one or another form of expression, that the evolutionary account of biological 'evil' may provide a consideration for theologians to take into account."[40] In other words, Ayala highlights that he is a scientist and not a theologian—implying that he is not qualified to answer these deeper questions.

38. For those who argue that God is still responsible for natural evil, Ayala responds, "Some would say . . . that because the world was created by God, God is ultimately responsible: God could have created a world without parasites or dysfunctionalities. Yes, others would answer, but a world of life with evolution is much more exciting; it is a creative world where new species arise, complex ecosystems come about, and humans have evolved. This account will not satisfy some people of faith and many unbelievers will surely find it less than cogent: a *Deus ex machina*. But I am suggesting that it may provide the beginning of an explanation for many people of faith, as well as for theologians" (Ayala, "Darwin and Intelligent Design," 765).

In addition to arguing that an evolving creation is more exciting than a static one, Ayala also contends that God could not have actualized a different world. Citing Keith Ward, he writes, "Could [God] not actualize a world wherein suffering is not a possibility? He could not, if any world complex and diverse enough to include rational and moral agents must necessarily include the possibility of suffering. . . . A world with the sorts of success and happiness in it that we occasionally experience is a world that necessarily contains the possibility of failure and misery" (Ayala, "Evolution Beyond Biology," 383). Contra Ayala, however, Russell argues, "The 'no choice' argument is based on a crucial underlying premise that is usually overlooked in discussion about evolution: it presupposes the laws of physics, or more generally the laws of nature, through which astrophysics, geology, chemistry, molecular and evolutionary biology, etc., work. Thus underlying the 'no choice' argument is the question of why our universe is characterized by these particular physical laws and not some other laws. Theologically this leads to the following point: Granted that if God were to create life by non-interventionist divine agency, God may have had 'no choice' other than to do so through neo-Darwinian evolution, assuming that the laws of nature are somehow 'given.' But the problem of 'God's choice' returns at a more fundamental level: since God created our universe *ex nihilo*, including its laws of nature, why did God choose to create *this* universe with *these* laws?" (Russell, "Is Evil Evolving?," 311).

39. Putz, "Love Actually," 349–50. Putz further writes, "The issue is exactly why God did not create a universe with different laws where death and suffering would have been impossible" (Putz, "Love Actually," 347).

40. Ayala, "Evolution Beyond Biology," 383.

Such a response is honest but problematic, since Ayala's main critique against ID is that ID advocates cannot provide adequate explanations for natural evil and suboptimal design in biology. If his account of evolutionary biology raises the same theological problems as ID, however, then his theological critique of ID loses its force. It seems, then, that both Ayala and ID advocates are in the same boat when it comes to explaining the problem of natural evil and suboptimal design in biology.

In this chapter, I have attempted to show that Ayala's theological critique against ID is problematic for several reasons. First, there are no good reasons to assume that a God with omni-attributes would refrain from creating organisms with suboptimal design. In fact, the task of natural theodicy, which Ayala undertakes, is to develop plausible explanations for natural evil given the existence of God. Second, the existence of design in biology is logically consistent with the existence of suboptimal design in biology. In other words, ID advocates are not claiming that every system in biology is designed, nor are they suggesting that any system is optimally designed. They merely contend that some systems in the natural world bear the marks of *actual* design, and therefore *intelligent* (or *conscious*) design is a plausible explanation for those systems. Third, Ayala's theodicy seems to face the same theological problems he raises against ID. Thus, if his theological critique of ID were sound, then it could also be used as a critique of Darwinian evolution.

On the other hand, if Ayala's theodicy does provide insights into the problem of suboptimal design in biology, then it is not clear why such a theodicy would be off limits for ID advocates. Behe, for example, charges ID critics with being guilty of either or thinking when it comes to evolution. He explains,

> One difficulty of writing a book questioning the sufficiency of Darwin's theory is that some people mistakenly conclude you're rejecting it in toto. It is time to get beyond either or thinking. Random mutation is a completely adequate explanation for some features of life, but not for others. This book looks for the line between the random and the nonrandom that defines the edge of evolution.[41]

As a leading thinker within the ID movement, Behe acknowledges the important role that randomness plays in biological evolution. Given this acknowledgement, Ayala's conclusion that a God with omni-attributes is more consistent with evolution than ID is unfounded, mainly because

41. Behe, *Edge of Evolution*, 14.

it relies upon a common misunderstanding of ID. This misunderstanding will be elucidated further as we consider Dembski's contribution to the ID project.

4

Defending Intelligent Design Scientifically

DEVELOPING AN OBJECTIVE APPROACH for recognizing design in nature has been a chief concern for many ID advocates. To date, William Dembski's has produced the most viable method for design detection, and this chapter sets out to articulate that method. A careful assessment of Dembki's work in this area is significant because it provides background for understanding where Ayala's theological critique against ID goes astray. I mentioned in earlier chapters that Ayala's definition of ID is not consistent with how leading ID advocates articulate their project. For example, Dembski explains that ID should be separated into four related but distinct tasks:

1. ID produces an objective method (SC) that distinguishes *intelligent causation* from *chance* or *necessity*.
2. ID produces scientific and/or mathematical arguments that demonstrate the inadequacy of Darwinian mechanisms to produce SC.
3. ID produces evidence that supports the claim that there are certain features in the natural world that cannot be explained by undirected natural forces.
4. ID produces a way of understanding divine action.

Ayala only focuses on the fourth task mentioned above, whereas most ID advocates emphasize the first three tasks.

In Dembski's first task, he contends that SC is an objective method that accurately distinguishes *intelligent causation* from *chance* or *necessity*. If he is correct, then his method could apply to various disciplines within science. His second and third tasks seek to demonstrate that SC applies specifically to the natural world. This is important because one might concede that SC is scientific in principle, but still maintain that it does not apply to biology.[1] To counter such an argument, Dembski challenges Darwinism and seeks to demonstrate that his method applies to the natural sciences.

Design and Science

Defending the claim that design belongs in science is difficult only when considering the natural sciences.[2] In disciplines like engineering or forensic science, discussions about design are incontrovertible. In disciplines like biology, however, similar discussions will be dismissed as mere creationism or anti-evolution propaganda.[3] Such dismissals persist, even though ID advocates frequently emphasize that ID is consistent with what Ayala calls *the fact of evolution*.[4] Before one defends ID as a scientific research

1. Dembski writes, "Claims that are refuted scientifically may be wrong, but they are not *necessarily* wrong—they cannot simply be dismissed out of hand. To see this, consider what would happen if microscopic examination revealed that every cell was inscribed with the phrase 'Made by Yahweh.' Of course cells don't have 'Made by Yahweh' inscribed on them, but that's not the point. The point is that we wouldn't know this unless we actually looked at cells under the microscope" (Dembski, "Science and Design," 21). Dembski argues in the preceding paragraph that the conclusion of ID may be incorrect, but that it should not be ruled out in principle.

2. By design, I am referring to *actual* design rather than *apparent* design. As mentioned previously, biologists typically recognize *apparent* design in biology. Richard Dawkins, for example, is frequently cited as saying, "Biology is the study of complicated things that give the appearance of having been designed for a purpose" (Dawkins, *Blind Watchmaker*, 4).

3. Yet Dembski argues that ID is neither: "It is not my aim to guarantee creationism. Design, as I develop it, cuts both ways and might just as well be used to defeat creationism by clarifying the superfluity of design in biology. My aim is not to find design in any one place but to open up possibilities for finding design as well as for shutting it down" (Dembski, "Third Mode of Explanation," 20). Furthermore, ID is not an attack on evolution, but on Darwinism, which will be demonstrated in the body of this chapter.

4. The fact of evolution refers to the idea of common descent. Dembski maintains that one could trace every step of the evolutionary process, demonstrate that all life originated from a common ancestor, and it would not refute ID. See Dembski and Wells, *Design of Life*, 140–42. See also chapter 2 for more details. Unfortunately, even though this point is often emphasized, ID thinkers obscure the issue in their writings. Dembski is no exception to this; in fact, he admits as much in his more recent work, *Being as Communion*. In a footnote, he admits that he can understand the confusion of critics when it comes to this issue: "Their criticisms are understandable because intelligent design advocates, myself included, haven't always been as clear as we might in our use of design terminology, not clearly distinguishing external design from intelligence or teleology

project, therefore, one must clarify what the project is and is not. ID is *not* a critique of biological evolution.[5] Instead, ID is fundamentally a claim that some events or objects bear the marks of actual design. Given this claim, many ID advocates argue that *design* should be considered an appropriate mode of explanation within science.

To establish ID's fundamental claim mentioned above, Dembski begins by defining three possible modes of causation: *chance*, *necessity*, and *design*. By necessity, Dembski refers to physical law-like relations between antecedent circumstances and consequent events. Necessity is distinguished from chance in that necessity generates events or objects that are highly probable. Chance, on the other hand, refers to blind and undirected contingency. Such contingencies produce events or objects with an intermediate degree of probability, suggesting that chance generates events or objects that are less probable than events or objects that are produced by necessity.

When articulating the concept of design, then, one must navigate between these other two modes of causation. Design is not chance, and it is not necessity. Rather, Dembski defines design as "directed contingency" or a superintending intelligence.[6] Design thus generates events or objects that are highly improbable, complex, and specified. After clarifying these possible modes of causation, Dembski claims that the gatekeepers of the natural sciences allow only chance and necessity when offering various modes of

---

more generally" (Dembski, *Being as Communion*, 59).

5. This is not to say that all ID advocates embrace evolution. ID historian, Thomas Woodward, traces the origin of the ID movement back to Michael Denton's *Evolution: A Theory in Crisis* and Phillip Johnson's *Darwin on Trial*, works that challenge *the fact of evolution*. See Woodward's *Doubts about Darwin* for details. Furthermore, Dembski and Wells also provide several critiques of common descent (Dembski and Wells, *Design of Life*, 60). One can understand, then, why critics pit ID against *the fact of evolution*. Upon a close evaluation of ID literature, however, I have concluded that the principles of ID are perfectly consistent with *the fact of evolution*.

6. To get a full explanation of his distinctions between necessity, chance, and design, see Dembski, "Signs of Intelligence," 172.

explanation.[7] This presumably puts ID proponents at a disadvantage when it comes to publishing their scientific research.[8]

Dembski then develops his case by clarifying how design is detected in everyday life. He refers to an arrangement of stones on a mountainside that spell "Welcome to Wales by British Railways" as an example.[9] Claiming that such an arrangement of stones was produced by design is certainly uncontroversial. By admitting this, however, we are agreeing with a fundamental aspect of Dembski's project—namely, that our design intuitions can be reliable. Dembski explains that most people recognize that chance and necessity (or the combination of the two) are implausible explanations for

---

7. I need to explicate further his proposed "third mode of explanation." When it comes to the physical sciences, Dembski contends that scientists unnecessarily restrict themselves to two modes of scientific explanation, namely, chance and necessity. Dembski defines necessity as an event that will almost always happen and chance as a probable occurrence of an event, but one that is also compatible with some other event happening. See Dembski, *Design Inference*, 8. In earlier works, Dembski uses the terms chance and regularity rather than chance and necessity. Throughout this book, I use the terms "chance" and "necessity." Dembski originally gets these categories from Jacques Monod. Monod argued that when scientists attempt to provide an explanation for any event or object, they must appeal only to chance, necessity, or a combination of the two to be considered legitimate science. For more details, see Dembski, *Design Revolution*, 9; Monod, *Chance and Necessity*.

8. Thus Dembski writes, "My aim in *The Design Inference* was to rehabilitate design. I argue that design is a legitimate and fundamental mode of scientific explanation on a par with chance and necessity" (Dembski, "Signs of Intelligence," 174).

9. Dembski, *Design Inference*, xi. Dembski also uses the examples of Mount Rushmore and rats running in a maze to illustrate this point. In the case of Mount Rushmore in western South Dakota, all three modes of explanation could be appropriate for explaining different features of the mountain. Necessity and chance provide a basic and general explanation for how the mountain originated in the first place. They do not, however, provide a good explanation for determining what caused four faces to emerge on the side of the mountain. To explain how the specific images of George Washington, Thomas Jefferson, Abraham Lincoln, and Theodore Roosevelt appear in the mountain, one needs a design explanation. To illustrate this point further, Dembski considers the ability of rats to run a maze. A psychologist studying the cognitive abilities of rats will construct a complicated maze and run a rat through it several times to see if the rat shows signs of learning. Each time the rat goes through the maze, if it appears to run through the maze quicker, taking less turns each time, the psychologist will likely determine that the rat is learning. This too is an application of ID, since the psychologist is using three modes of causal explanation to explain the rat's behavior. Some of the turns made by the rat may be determined by chance, but, as future experiments are conducted, the psychologist will use design as a mode of explanation to explain the rat's ability to learn.

the aforementioned arrangement. And if chance and necessity are implausible, then the only alternative explanation is design.[10]

Dembski's stone illustration shows that design inferences are common in human experience. His goal in the illustration is to illuminate the process one subjectively works through in such inferences, and then articulate how such a process could be made objective.[11] He does this by revealing specific characteristics in the arrangement of stones that cause one to rightly infer design, and then notes that the arrangement is highly improbable.[12] Dembski stresses that improbability by itself is not sufficient for detecting design, since any arrangement of stones would be highly improbable. He does argue, however, that a high enough degree of improbability eliminates necessity. This reduces our modes of explanation to either a chance explanation or a design explanation.[13]

The next step in Dembski's method is to show how the particular arrangement of stones conforms to a pattern.[14] He notes that chance is able

10. By appealing to design in such cases, one should note that this is not an argument for a specific designer, but a general designer. This means that appeals to design do not necessarily indicate who the designer was. When it comes to an English sentence like "Welcome to Wales by British Railways" one reasonably can infer that the designer was human. Of course, this inference is not certain. The designer could be an extraterrestrial intelligence who mastered the English language. The designer could also be supernatural. Such options seem unlikely, but the point is that inferences to design do not attempt to identify the designing agent.

11. Dembski explains that he does not wish to simply *feel* like an event or object is designed. He wants to put numerical values on what constitutes a highly improbable event or object and thus make his design inference a non-subjective criteria (Dembski, *Design Inference*, 5).

12. Dembski writes, "What counts as a small probability depends on an inquirer's interests and context for eliminating chance. Social scientists who set their alpha level at .05 or .01 are less stringent than criminal courts that establish guilt to a moral certainty and beyond reasonable doubt, and these in turn are less stringent than inflationary cosmologists as they account for the relative flatness of spacetime" (Dembski, *Design Inference*, 6–7).

13. Dembski also notes that a designer can produce an event that is highly probable and thus disguise his or her design. This is not a problem for Dembski's method, however, because his goal is to clarify when design can be correctly inferred. Certainly, there can be examples that are falsely attributed to chance or necessity due to the stealth nature of some designers.

14. Dembski writes, "By pattern we shall mean any description that corresponds uniquely to some prescribed event" (Dembski, *Design Inference*, 136). Dembski notes that there are two types of patterns. One is specification, where non-*ad hoc* patterns can legitimately be used to eliminate chance and warrant a design inference. The other is fabrication, where patterns are invented afterward and imposed on the data. An archer who

to generate some patterns and that chance and necessity working together might even produce fairly complex patterns. The crucial question for Dembski, though, is whether the pattern of stones conforms to the right sort of pattern to eliminate chance.[15] He calls this *right sort of pattern* "specification" and argues that if a pattern is specified for a particular purpose, then one can rightly eliminate chance as well as the combination of chance and necessity. A proper elimination of chance and necessity, therefore, allows one to objectively infer design, and Dembski maintains that people intuitively and rightly make such inferences all the time.[16]

Broadly speaking, Dembski claims that his project has several scientific applications. In the preface of *The Design Inference*, he writes that the scope of his work applies to "forensic scientists, SETI researchers, insurance fraud investigators, debunkers of psychic phenomena, origins-of-life researchers, intellectual property attorneys, investigators of data falsification, cryptographers, parapsychology researchers, and programmers of (pseudo-) random number generators."[17] One can appreciate the scientific significance of Dembski's method, therefore, even if one does not consider it appropriate for biology.[18] In each application provided above, Dembski contends that design is the third mode of explanation that appropriately belongs within scientific discourse.[19]

---

shoots an arrow and only afterwards draws the target would constitute an improbable event that conforms to a particular pattern. That pattern is *ad hoc* and would constitute a fabrication (Dembski, *Design Inference*, 5, 13).

15. Dembski, *Design Inference*, xi.

16. Dembski notes that the concepts of complexity and specification are "well-defined information-theoretic concepts" (Dembski, "Evolutionary Algorithms," 94).

17. Dembski, *Design Inference*, xii. Some argue, however, that Dembski is wrong to consider such applications subsets of ID. Gary Hurd, for example, argues that forensic science "is like all other historical sciences in that practitioners rely on analogy, direct observation, replication, and the applications of basic sciences" (Hurd, "Explanatory Filter, Archaeology, Forensics," 116). He further argues that Dembski's ID offers nothing to forensics, sense it does not have the resources to determine specific causes of death, and it cannot always distinguish between events where suicide or accident are equally likely. The problem with Hurd's criticisms is that they try to get more out of the explanatory filter than Dembski intends. As I show later in this chapter, Dembski's filter applies to adjudicating between different *modes of explanation*, not between specific explanations.

18. Recognizing the various applications for Dembski's method should alleviate the fear that ID is simply a repackaged form of biblical creationism.

19. Dembski, "Third Mode of Explanation," 17. Here Dembski argues that philosophers and scientists throughout history have debated the applicability of each of these modes. Epicureans liked chance, Stoics emphasized design and necessity, Moses

Detecting Design

Dembski then develops different ways to articulate an objective inference to design. Most notable is his notion of SC or CSI, which is expressed using his Explanatory Filter. The Explanatory Filter is a flow chart that elucidates how one should distinguish between necessity, chance, and design. The chart begins with a question about contingency.[20] When considering any particular event E, the inquirer must ask whether E is a highly probable event? If the answer is yes, then E is not a contingent event, but rather a product of necessity. Dembski illustrates this point by considering the rolling of a weighted die. The probability of rolling a six on a fair die is one in six. If the die is weighted in favor of rolling a six, however, the probability increases. Rolling a six with a weighted die thus can be explained by an appeal to necessity rather than chance.

If one discovers that event E is not highly probable, then one can proceed to step 2 and ask the complexity question. Is event E an intermediately probable (IP) event? If yes, then the event is not complex and should therefore be considered a product of chance. Rolling a six using a fair die illustrates this seconds step. Since any role can be attributed to a one in six chance, rolling a six (event E) should also be considered a product of chance.

Suppose one discovers that event E does not have an intermediate level of probability. Dembski argues that one should proceed to step 3 and ask the specification question. Is event E an event with small probability *and* specification (sp/SP)? If yes, then one should consider E a product of design. Dembski calls this principle the Law of Small Probability, in which specified events of small probability do not occur by chance. He formulates an argument for this principle as follows:[21]

- Premise 1: E has occurred.
- Premise 2: E is specified.
- Premise 3: If E is due to chance, then E has small probability.

Maimonides emphasized design, Newton saw both necessity and design as legitimate explanations, and Laplace sought to rid astronomy of design.

20. There are a few different versions of the Explanatory Filter; Dembski's idea has developed over time.

21. Dembski, *Design Inference*, 48.

- Premise 4: Specified events of small probability do not occur by chance.
- Premise 5: E is not due to a necessity.
- Premise 6: E is due either to necessity, chance, or design.
- Conclusion: E is due to design.

The formulation of this argument regards design as the elimination of chance, and chance is the elimination of necessity.[22]

A common criticism of Dembski's Explanatory Filter is that it represents an argument from ignorance. Wesley Elsberry, for example, writes,

> Dembski objects to critics' characterizing his [Explanatory Filter] as an argument from ignorance. In response to such claims, he responds that arguments from ignorance have a logical structure of "not X, therefore Y," and that applying his [Explanatory Filter] in analysis requires considerable knowledge. It is curious that Dembski himself lays out the "not X, therefore Y" structure of a fallacious argument as if his [Explanatory Filter] were in some respect different. It is clear from *The Design Inference* and *No Free Lunch*, however, that Dembski's [Explanatory Filter] is a deductive eliminative argument that demands acceptance of design when regularity [or necessity] and chance hypotheses of causation have been excluded. His formulation of design from *The Design Inference*, which has not been retracted, reads as follows: des (E) = def ~reg(E) & ($\forall$H) ~ch (E|H).[23]

Elsberry concludes, "Simply stated, this equation says that an event is due to design if it is not due to regularity [necessity] and also is not due to chance, for all relevant chance hypotheses."[24] Thus Dembski's argument is presumably portrayed as a simple argument from ignorance, rather than a positive method for detecting design.

---

22. Dembski writes, "We may think of design and chance as competing modes of explanation for which design prevails once chance is exhausted. In eliminating chance, the design inference eliminates not just a single chance hypothesis, but all relevant chance hypotheses" (Dembski, *Design Inference*, 8). He further distinguishes the design inference (DI) from Bayes's theorem. Whereas Bayes's theorem attempts to confirm hypotheses, DI does not. There is no design hypothesis; rather, DI is purely eliminative (Dembski, *Design Inference*, 68).

23. Elsberry, "Logic and Math," 259–60.

24. Elsberry, "Logic and Math," 260.

Contra Elsberry, Dembski claims that his argument is not an argument from ignorance because it involves formulating and ascribing mathematical probabilities to particular events and objects set against relevant background information. He explains,

> We need to know quite a bit to estimate likelihoods. It seems, therefore, inappropriate to describe what we are doing when we estimate likelihoods as "measuring ignorance." Ignorance typically connotes a lack of knowledge that can be remedied, and should have been remedied, but wasn't because of negligence. Estimating likelihoods in the light of relevant background information is nothing of the sort. When estimating likelihoods, we have typically remedied as much ignorance as we are able. What uncertainty remains is due not to negligence, but to the difficulties inherent in ruling out alternate possibilities.[25]

Dembski further objects to calling this process an argument from ignorance because it would entail that any appeals to design (including human design) could also be attributed to ignorance. The relevant question for Dembski, then, is not related to the particular structure of his argument. The relevant question is whether one can justify the Law of Small Probability.[26]

In *The Design Inference*, Dembski defends the Law of Small Probability using probability and complexity theory.[27] He explains that complexity theory measures the difficulty of a problem to solve problem Q given certain resources R. He refers to the complexity of a padlock to illustrate this idea, stating that it would be difficult for a person to open a padlock (Q) if she does not know the combination (R). She could certainly try, but given her resources, she will likely fail.

On the other hand, it would not be difficult for a person to open a padlock (Q), assuming that she *does* know the combination (R). This illustrates the simple principle that difficulty goes up or down relative to the relevant resources—which can be denoted by D (Q|R), with the range of numbers being 0 to ∞. This means that D (Q|R) = 0 indicates minimal difficulty, whereas D (Q|R) = ∞ indicates maximal difficulty.[28] Articulating

---

25. Dembski, *Design Inference*, 82.

26. Dembski defines this law as the idea that "specified events of small probability do not occur by chance" (Dembski, *Design Inference*, 5).

27. Dembski, *Design Inference*, 92.

28. Dembski, *Design Inference*, 100.

this formula makes the notion of complexity tangible, and, by providing a numerical method, Dembski demonstrates that his design inference is not merely subjective.

Furthermore, Dembski's padlock example demonstrates how the elimination of chance and necessity is a responsible form of argumentation. The reason it is difficult for a person to open a padlock (Q) given that she does *not* know the combination, is because she would be relying only upon chance and necessity (R). And neither chance nor necessity nor the combination of the two have resources needed to easily open a padlock. If one knows the combination, however, then one can easily open the padlock because one is then relying upon design. Thus, when one reasons that the lock must have been opened by design, one is not arguing on the basis of ignorance. Rather, one is basing this intuition upon the knowledge of resources needed to accomplish the task of unlocking the padlock with minimal difficulty.[29]

Another objection to Dembski's method is found in the anthropic principle, which he calls the *inventing probabilistic resources* objection.[30] In short, this objection states that if an event X seems incredibly improbable given our current understanding of the world, then one must introduce an additional chance hypothesis to increase one's probabilistic resources.[31] To

---

29. Dembski provides details in *Design Inference* that are too involved to cover in this chapter. He specifically seeks to demonstrate that specificity and highly improbable events can be quantified, even if there is an aspect of subjectivity. Dembski notes that all statistics involve subjectivity when applying numerical values to particular events: "To define probability as the best available estimate of likelihood is therefore to embrace fallibilism and progressivism as ineliminable aspects of probability. How we determine the best available estimate of the likelihood of an event is in the end a function of our accumulated knowledge for dealing with uncertainty. Such knowledge consists of norms and practices that are constantly being corrected and refined. Such knowledge arises within a community of discourse and reflects the practices of those judged by the community as expert in the estimation of likelihoods. As the best available estimate of the likelihood of an event in the light of relevant background information, the probability of an event is the estimate on which this group of experts agrees. What gets assigned as the probability of an event is therefore historically contingent. I offer no algorithm for assigning practical purposes it suffices that a community of discourse can settles on a fixed estimate of likelihood" (Dembski, *Design Inference*, 87).

30. Dembski, *No Free Lunch*, 85.

31. Dembski notes that astrophysicist Brandon Carter coined the term in 1970: "In its original formulation, the Anthropic Principle merely states that the physical laws and fundamental constants that structure the universe must be compatible with human observes. Since human observes exist, the principle is obviously true" (Dembski, "Design Argument," 339).

understand this objection, think of the improbability of winning the lottery. The chances of any particular person winning the lottery are incredibly low. When someone does win the lottery, however, we do not automatically infer that the lottery was rigged (or designed). Instead, we consider the full extent of our probabilistic resources by recognizing that someone is bound to win the lottery by chance, given that there are millions of people who play the lottery every week.

One could use this lottery illustration to explain why the improbability of life originating on earth is unsurprising. Yes, given our current knowledge and understanding of the universe, the odds of life existing on our planet is astronomically low. But if one considers the cosmic context, then one should recognize that life is bound to appear somewhere in the universe. And when life does appear, the proper conclusion is simply that one tiny planet within an immense universe won the cosmic lottery. There is nothing surprising about such an event. Dawkins explains,

> The anthropic alternative to the design hypothesis is statistical. Scientists invoke the magic of large numbers. It has been estimated that there are between 1 billion to 30 billion planets in our galaxy, and about 100 billion galaxies in the universe. Knocking a few noughts off for reasons of ordinary prudence, a billion billion is a conservative estimate of the number of available planets in the universe. Now, suppose the origin of life, the spontaneous arising of something equivalent to DNA, really was a quite staggeringly improbable event. Suppose it was so improbable as to occur on only one in a billion planets. A grant-giving body would laugh at any chemist who admitted that the chance of his proposed research succeeding was only one in a hundred. But here we are talking about odds of one in a billion. And yet . . . even with such absurdly long odds, life will still have arisen on a billion planets—of which Earth, of course, is one.[32]

Many have extended Dawkins's argument by further contending that our universe is just one among a potentially infinite number of universes.[33]

---

32. Dawkins, *God Delusion*, 165

33. Lawrence Krauss makes this argument when he writes, "Our universe is so vast that, as I have emphasized, something that is not impossible is virtually guaranteed to occur somewhere within it. Rare events happen all the time. You might wonder whether the same principle applies to the possibility of many universes, or a *multiverse*, as the idea is now known" (Krauss, *Universe from Nothing*, 126).

Given such large probabilistic resources, therefore, many find it easy to conceive of life originating by pure chance.

Dembski is unimpressed with this kind of reasoning, claiming that it merely invents probabilistic resources. He calls these unlimited probabilistic resources "Z-factors," arguing that they

> allow us to explain absolutely everything by reference to chance—not just natural objects that actually did result by chance and not just natural objects that look designed, but also all artificial objects that are in fact designed. In effect, unlimited probabilistic resources collapse the distinction between apparent design and actual design and make it impossible to attribute anything with confidence to actual design.[34]

He further asserts that there is "no principled way to discriminate between using unlimited probabilistic resources to retain chance and using specified complexity to eliminate chance."[35] In other words, those who rely on chance Z-factors have predetermined that design is not an appropriate Z-factor. For them, the only appropriate Z-factors are those consistent with an unguided and nonteleological perspective on reality. But if one takes this approach to eliminating design as an appropriate mode of explanation, then everything can reasonably be attributed to chance—including rock formations that spell "Welcome to Wales by British Railways." While such a formation is indeed highly improbable, given the vastness of our universe (and perhaps the multiverse), such formations are bound to eventually arise by chance.

Dembski's project up until this point is insightful and useful, but I should pause briefly to address whether Dembski is pursuing a scientific research project. I am currently undecided as to whether certain aspects of ID should be considered scientific. What is clear to me, however, is that Dembski's form of argumentation is similar to the form of argumentation utilized by Ayala and other ID critics. As seen in chapter 2, Ayala maintains that Darwin's great accomplishment was to provide a "scientific explanation of design."[36] Was this accomplishment a *scientific* accomplishment? Or was it a *philosophical*? From my perspective, it does not matter. What does matter is the principle of consistency—that is, if one thinks Ayala's arguments are scientific in form, then one should also think that Dembski's

---

34. Dembski, *No Free Lunch*, 93.
35. Dembski, *No Free Lunch*, 96.
36. Ayala, *Big Questions*, 47.

arguments are scientific in form. Likewise, if one thinks Dembski is *merely* doing philosophy, then one should also think that Ayala is *merely* doing philosophy. In other words, I am not concerned about articulating a clear demarcation of science; rather I am concerned about treating each thinker in a consistent manner.

Design Inferences in Biology

The next relevant question is whether design inferences can, in principle, apply to biology. Dembski claims that they do and that they challenge the prevailing Darwinian perspective on life.[37] At this stage in Dembski's project, ID represents an alternative approach to evolution, contending that, "intelligent causes are necessary to explain the complex, information-rich structures of biology and that these causes are empirically detectable."[38] This approach rejects the influence naturalism has on biology, though it does not deny the reality of all natural processes. Dembski agrees, for example, that random mutation and natural selection play a major role in evolutionary development, but he also argues that such mechanisms are not sufficient to explain the whole diversity of life.[39] And if random mutation (chance) and natural selection (necessity) are not sufficient, then Dembski

---

37. Dembski, "Design Argument," 341. Dembski treats Darwinism as a worldview, and thus must be distinguished from the theory of evolution.

38. Dembski, "Design Argument," 341. Dembski explains how this is different than Darwinism: "Evolutionary biology teaches that all biological complexity is the result of material mechanisms. These include, principally, the Darwinian mechanism of natural selection and random variation, but they also include other mechanisms (symbiogenesis, gene transfer, genetic drift, the action of regulatory genes in development, self-organizational processes, etc.). These mechanisms are just that: mindless material mechanisms that do what they do irrespective of intelligence. To be sure, mechanisms can be programmed by an intelligence. But any such intelligent programming of evolutionary mechanisms is not properly part of evolutionary biology. Intelligent Design, by contrast teaches that biological complexity is not exclusively the result of material mechanisms but also requires intelligence, where the intelligence in question is not reducible to such mechanisms" (Dembski, "Logical Underpinnings of Intelligent Design," 323).

39. Dembski explains, "Darwinism is really two claims. The less crucial claim is that all organisms trace their lineage back to a universal common ancestor. . . . This claim is referred to as 'common descent.' Although evolutionary biology is committed to common descent, that is not its central claim. Rather, the central claim of evolutionary biology is that an unguided physical process can account for the emergence of all biological complexity and diversity. Filling in the details of that process remains a matter for debate among evolutionary biologists" (Dembski, "Myths of Darwinism," xx).

maintains that teleological explanations (design) should be acknowledged in biology. He further explains,

> For many in the scientific community, natural causes are at heart nonteleological and therefore unintelligent. Natural causes, when suitably coordinated, may exhibit intelligence. Thus, animals might be viewed as purely natural objects that act as intelligent causes to achieve ends. But the teleology they exhibit is, from a naturalistic perspective, the result of a long and blind evolutionary process whose nuts-and-bolts causal processes are nonteleological. Given naturalism, natural causes bring about intelligent causes but are not themselves intelligent. On this view, intelligent causes are always reducible to nonteleological natural causes, ultimately to the motions and interactions of particles governed by forces of attraction and repulsion.[40]

Dembski highlights a crucial issue in this paragraph. Very few scientists will deny all examples of teleology. Even naturalists explain rock formations that spell English sentences by appealing to design. Dembski argues, however, that naturalists are being inconsistent, given that any example of teleology, within a naturalistic worldview, would ultimately be reduced to deeper *nonteleological* physical processes. This means that intelligence—whether human or animal intelligence—is fundamentally the result of blind evolutionary processes.[41] Thus Darwinism (the combination of naturalism and evolution) must explain all examples of design in the world by reducing them to chance and necessity or the combination of the two. When this conclusion is taken seriously, it undermines the very intelligence needed to make scientific discoveries in the first place.[42]

In addition to the self-defeating nature Darwinism, Dembski further contends that ID is relevant for biology because it provides a better explanation for biological information:[43]

---

40. Dembski and Marks, "Life's Conservation Law," 363.

41. Dembski and Marks, "Life's Conservation Law," 364.

42. Similar arguments have been made by various Christian and non-Christian thinkers. Alvin Plantinga, for example, provides a persuasive defense of this argument in his evolutionary argument against naturalism (EAAN). For details, see Plantinga, *Where the Conflict Really Lies*. See also Nagel, *Mind & Cosmos*.

43. Particularly, Dembski has in mind the kind of information that is represented by SC. If there are biological examples that exhibit SC, Dembski argues that natural causes would not be able to explain them. This is not just the case due to the fact of being able to provide an example of natural causes generating SC, but it is true in principle. He distinguishes SC from Shannon information, which is more concerned with determining

> The central issue in the scientific debate over intelligent design and biological evolution can therefore be stated as follows: Is nature complete in the sense of possessing all the resources it needs to bring about the information-rich biological structures we see around us, or does nature also require some contribution of design to bring about those structures? Darwinian naturalism argues that nature is able to create all its own information and is therefore complete. Intelligent design, by contrast, argues that nature is merely able to re-express existing information and is therefore incomplete.[44]

The case for ID in biology, then, is a case regarding the nature and origin of biological information. Information is presumably what distinguishes the organic from the inorganic, and Dembski claims that naturalistic mechanisms are not able to produce the information needed to create life.[45] To argue for ID in biology, therefore, one must demonstrate that neither chance nor necessity nor the combination of the two can bridge the gap between the organic and inorganic worlds. Dembski claims that ID advocates have offered such demonstrations, and concludes that the

---

the improbability or complexity of a particular string of characters. Though SC takes Shannon's information into account, it also considers the patterning or significance of the characters in question.

44. Dembski and Marks, "Life's Conservation Law," 362. Dembski utilizes Behe's concept of irreducible complexity in organisms like the bacterial flagellum. He argues that Darwinian mechanisms cannot produce such structures: "Given a pre-specified goal, selection has no difficulty producing irreducibly complex systems. But the selection operating in biology is Darwinian natural selection. And by definition this form of selection operates without goals, has neither plan nor purpose, and is wholly undirected. The great appeal of Darwin's selection mechanism was, after all, that it would eliminate teleology from biology. Yet by making selection an undirected process, Darwin drastically reduced the type of complexity biological systems could manifest. Henceforth biological systems could manifest only cumulative complexity, not irreducible complexity" (Dembski, "Science and Design," 25).

45. Again, Dembski is not suggesting that naturalistic mechanisms are irrelevant for all biological structures: "Not all biological structures or arrangements are equally relevant to deciding whether life is designed. For instance, Darwin's mechanism of natural selection acting on random variation is responsible for certain features of biological systems. Antibiotic resistance in bacteria and insecticide resistance in insects can be readily accounted for in terms of the Darwinian mechanism" (Dembski, *Design Revolution*, 139–40). Moreover, Dembski overemphasizes the point that ID does not negate naturalistic mechanisms, and he illustrates the point by referencing the design of a rusted old automobile, which bears the marks of design (engineering) and natural forces (weathering and corrosion). Similarly, biological systems could be expected to reveal design, chance, and necessity.

great myth of Darwinism is that biological information can be purchased without intelligence.[46]

Ayala's project, it seems, represents the Darwinian idea that Dembski is critiquing. As seen in chapter 2, Ayala argues that natural selection working upon random mutations is capable of explaining the totality of life. This implies that chance and necessity do have sufficient resources to generate biological information. Ayala writes,

> Chance is . . . an integral part of the evolutionary process. The mutations that yield the hereditary variations available to natural selection arise at random, independently of whether they are beneficial or harmful to their carriers. This random process (as well as others that come to play in the great theatre of life) is counteracted by natural selection, which preserves what is useful and eliminates the harmful. Without mutation, evolution could not happen because there would be no variations that could be differentially conveyed from one to another generation. Without natural selection, the mutation process would yield disorganization and extinction because most mutations are disadvantageous. Mutation and selection have jointly driven the marvelous process that starting from microscopic organisms has spurted orchids, birds and humans.[47]

He continues,

> The theory of evolution manifests chance and necessity jointly intertwined in the stuff of life; randomness and determinism interlocked in a natural process that has brought forth the most complex, diverse, and beautiful entities in the universe: the organisms that populate the earth, including humans who think and love, endowed with free will and creative powers, and able to analyze the process of evolution itself that brought them into

---

46. Dembski, *No Free Lunch*, 148. Dembski further argues that Darwin's main claim to fame is that he supposedly provided a mechanism that could create information without the need for intelligence (Dembski and Marks, "Life's Conservation Law," 361). Elsewhere, he writes, "Darwin's claim to fame was to propose natural selection as a designer substitute. But natural selection is no substitute for intelligent coordination. All natural selection does is narrow the variability of incidental change by weeding out the less fit. What's more, it acts on the spur of the moment, based solely on what the environment at present deems fit, and thus without any foresight of future possibilities. And yet this blind process, when coupled with another blind process (incidental change), is supposed to produce designs that exceed the capacities of any designers in our experience" (Dembski, "Myths of Darwinism," xxi).

47. Ayala, "Chance and Necessity," 238.

existence. This was Darwin's fundamental discovery, that there is a natural process that is creative, though not conscious.[48]

For Ayala, chance and necessity alone can produce any facet of biological complexity. This even includes the biological complexity needed to analyze the process of evolution that brought conscious analysers into existence. Dembski objects to this idea, stating that no one has produced a viable theoretical model to substantiate Ayala's claim. He then reviews and critiques various models that have been proposed, concluding that such proposals support ID more than Darwinian evolution.

One such proposal is Richard Dawkins's weasel program—an evolutionary algorithm introduced in *The Blind Watchmaker*. This algorithm is just one model that attempts to illustrate how random mutation and natural selections might produce complex information, such as the Shakespearian sentence, METHINKS IT IS LIKE A WEASEL.[49] Dawkins explains that his algorithm allows one to enter a random sequence of 28 letters (WDLMNLT DTJBKWIRZREZLMQCOP) into a computer program designed to simulate the effects of natural selection acting upon random mutations.[50] He details the procedures of this program as follows:

> [The sequence of letters] "breeds from" a random phrase. It duplicates it repeatedly, but with a certain chance of random error—"mutation"—in the copying. The computer examines the mutant nonsense phrases, the progeny of the original phrase, and chooses the one which, *however slightly*, most resembles the target phrase, METHINKS IT IS LIKE A WEASEL. In this instance the winning phrase of the next "generation" happened to be: WDLTMNLT DTJBSWIRZREZLMQCOP. Not an obvious improvement! But the procedure is repeated, again mutant "progeny" are "bred from" the phrase, and a new "winner" is chosen. This goes on, generation after generation.[51]

According to one particular run, Dawkins notes that the random sequence evolved into the target sequence in just 43 generations. This presumably shows that the ingredients of time, chance, and necessity can all work together to produce an example of complex and specified information. No design is needed.

48. Ayala, "Chance and Necessity," 238.
49. Dawkins, *Blind Watchmaker*, 66.
50. Dawkins, *Blind Watchmaker*, 68.
51. Dawkins, *Blind Watchmaker*, 68

Dembski notes, however, that Dawkins's algorithm provides a theoretical model of evolution that actually favors ID. He writes,

> Does Dawkins's evolutionary algorithm demonstrate the power of the Darwinian mechanism to create biological information? No. Clearly, the algorithm was stacked to produce the outcome Dawkins was after. Indeed, because the algorithm was constantly gauging the degree of difference between the current sequence from the target sequence, the very thing that the algorithm was supposed to create (i.e., the target sequence METHINKS IT IS LIKE A WEASEL) was in fact smuggled into the algorithm from the start.[52]

In other words, the Weasel algorithm demonstrates that evolution needs four ingredients to produce a line of Shakespeare: time, chance, necessity, *and design*. Thus Dawkins's model does not support Darwinism, it supports ID.[53]

Evaluating Scientific Critiques of Design

In chapter 2, I showed that Ayala's first four scientific critiques center on the claim that ID is in conflict with evolution. A careful reading of

---

52. Dembski and Marks, "Life's Conservation Law," 366–67.

53. Dembski offers a more specific refutation of Dawkins: "In WEASEL, Dawkins starts with a blind search whose probability of success in one query is roughly 1 in 1040. This is p. He then implements an alternative search (his evolutionary algorithm) whose probability of success in a few dozen queries is close to 1. This is q. Dawkins leaves the discussion hanging, as though having furnished an evolutionary algorithm that locates the target phrase with high probability (which we are calling S), he has demonstrated the power of Darwinian processes. But in fact all he has done is shifted the problem of locating the target elsewhere. . . . Thus, in furnishing an alternative search whose probability of success is q, he incurred a probability of cost p of finding the right fitness function, which coincides (not coincidentally) with the original improbability of the null search finding the target. The information problem that Dawkins purported to solve is therefore left completely unresolved" (Dembski and Marks, "Life's Conservation Law," 372). Dembski also considers other evolutionary algorithms, such as Christoph Adami's AVIDA, Thomas Ray's Tierra, and Thomas Schneider's *ev*. Each of these programs are meant to demonstrate the power of natural selection and random mutation. Dembski argues that the main problem with these programs is that they "capitalize on ignorance of how information works. The information hidden in them can be uncovered through a quantity we call *active information*. Active information is to information accounting what the balance sheet is to financial accounting" (Dembski and Marks, "Life's Conservation Law," 372). Additionally, Dembski refers to MESA, Mendel's Accountant, and MutationWorks as ID-produced programs meant to demonstrate the inefficiency of the Darwinian mechanism to produce SC.

Dembski's work demonstrates that this is not true.[54] That is, ID is in conflict with Darwinism, but not evolution per se. Ayala's fifth scientific critique, however, does provide a direct challenge to ID, since it offers a specific response to Dembski's design inference. For the remainder of this chapter, I will assess each of Ayala's scientific critiques in light of Dembski's contributions to ID.

The Paley-to-Darwin History

Ayala started his critique against ID by arguing that Darwin overturned the design argument that was articulated and popularized by Paley, and thus completed the scientific revolution.[55] He further maintains that the modern ID movement is simply a rehashing of Paley's design argument. Not surprisingly, Dembski's retelling the Paley-to-Darwin history differs from Ayala's account. For Ayala, Christian theologians—desiring to produce a natural theology—invented design arguments to demonstrate the existence of God. Dembski, however, shows that design arguments originated well before the rise of Christianity. He explains,

> Full-fledged design arguments have been available since classical times. Both Aristotle's (384–322 BC) final causes and the Stoics' seminal reason were types of intelligent causation inferred

---

54. Dembski provides a helpful illustration regarding how natural processes and design could work together: "Imagine an embossed sign that reads *Eat at Frank's* falls over in a snowstorm and leaves the mirror image of *Eat at Frank's* embedded in the snow. Granted, the sign fell over as a result of undirected natural forces, and on that basis the impression the sign left in the snow would not be attributed to design by the [explanatory] filter. Nonetheless, there is a relevant event whose design needs to be assessed, namely, the structuring of the embossed image (whether in the snow or on the sign). This event must be referred back to the activity of the sign's maker, and the Explanatory Filter properly ascribes it to design. Natural forces can serve as conduits of design. As a result, a simple inspection of those natural forces may turn up no evidence of design. Often one must look deeper" (Dembski, *Design Revolution*, 91).

55. Dembski references Ayala on this point in a discussion he had with Michael Ruse: "I think we need to be very clear what we are talking about with evolutionary theory. We're not talking about a guided form of evolution in which God or some intelligence was controlling the process in some substantive way where we can see clear, empirically detectable marks of that intelligence. What is meant by evolution is a process that, for all our scientific investigation can reveal, did not require any intelligence. Francisco Ayala, for instance, describes what he calls 'Darwin's Greatest Achievement' as showing how you get the organization of living forms apart from any design or creative intelligence" (Dembski and Ruse, "Intelligent Design," 13).

at least in part from the apparent order and purposiveness of the physical world. For example, in *De natura deorum* (*On the Nature of the Gods*), Cicero (106–43 BC) writes: "When we see something moved by machinery, like an orrery or clock ... we do not doubt that these contrivances are the work of reason; when therefore we behold the whole compass with perfect regularity the annual changes of the seasons with absolute safety and security for all things, how can we doubt that all this is effected not merely by reason, but by a reason that is transcendent and divine?" (Cicero 1933, 217–19).[56]

Dembski further articulates Aristotle's distinctions between material, efficient, formal, and final causes by reflecting on Michelangelo's *Statue of David*. The material cause of the statue is the marble used in its construction. The efficient cause is chipping the marble slab with a hammer and chisel. The formal cause is that the structure represents David rather than a random block of marble. The final cause is the purpose of the statue, namely, to produce a work of art.[57] These four causes, Dembski notes, were widely discussed in natural philosophy prior to the development of natural theology.

Dembski, therefore, seeks to provide a more comprehensive narrative of the history of teleological reasoning. He emphasizes the fact that both Christians and non-Christians utilized the notion of teleology when reasoning about the natural world, and that this began to change only after Francis Bacon (1561–1626) proposed that science should ignore Aristotle's concepts of formal and final causation. Bacon's proposal, according to Dembski, was not based upon new scientific discoveries; rather it signified an arbitrary change regarding the rules of science.[58] Reinstating the notion of design in

---

56. Dembski, "Design Argument," 336.

57. Dembski, "Third Mode of Explanation," 20–21.

58. Dembski notes further that Jacques Monod's *Chance and Necessity* represents a modern version of Bacon's thought. For Monod, chance and necessity alone "suffice to account for every aspect of the universe" (Dembski, "Third Mode of Explanation," 21). Dembski also writes, "Throughout the centuries theologians have argued that nature exhibits features that nature itself cannot explain but that instead require an intelligence beyond nature. From church fathers like Minucius Felix and Gregory of Nazianzus (third and fourth centuries) to medieval scholars like Moses Maimonides and Thomas Aquinas (twelfth and thirteenth centuries) to Reformed thinkers like Thomas Reid and Charles Hodge (eighteenth and nineteenth centuries), we find theologians making design arguments, arguing from the data of nature to an intelligence that transcends nature. Design arguments are old hat. Indeed, design arguments continue to be a staple of philosophy and religion courses. The most famous of the design arguments is William Paley's watchmaker argument" (Dembski, "What Every Theologian Should Know," 223).

science, therefore, is not return to natural theology. Instead, Dembski argues that it is a return to the broader tradition of natural philosophy—the very tradition that gave rise to modern science.

Given this historical context, Dembski then maintains that while Paley's *Natural Theology* and the central claims of ID are related, they are also distinct academic pursuits:

> It is the empirical detectability of intelligent causes that renders intelligent design a fully scientific theory and distinguishes it from the design arguments of philosophers, or what has traditionally been called *natural theology*. Natural theology reasons from the data of nature directly to the existence and attributes of God. . . . Perhaps the weakest part of Paley's *Natural Theology* was his closing chapter where he sings the praises of nature's delicate balance and how only a beneficent deity could have arranged so happy a creation. Darwin turned this argument on its head, focusing instead on the brutality of nature and seeing anything but the hand of a beneficent deity.[59]

Dembski interestingly agrees with Ayala, contending that Darwin turned Paley's argument on its head regarding the brutality of nature. He even agrees that Darwin delivered the greatest blow to the design argument.[60] What makes ID different than Paley's natural theology, however, is ID's theological neutrality. Dembski explains that ID "resists speculating about the nature, moral character or purposes of [the designer]."[61] This means that the brutality of nature does not negate the reality of teleology. At best, it undermines the goodness of the designer. Such a complaint, however, is a theological rather than a scientific complaint.

The "Problem" of Evolution

As mentioned previously, ID is perfectly compatible with *the fact of evolution*. To quote Dembski again: "Logically, intelligent design is compatible with everything from utterly discontinuous creation (e.g., God intervening at every conceivable point to create new species) to the most far-ranging evolution (e.g., God seamlessly melding all organisms together into one

---

59. Dembski, "What Every Theologian Should Know," 225.
60. Dembski, "Design Argument," 338–39.
61. Dembski, "What Every Theologian Should Know," 225.

great tree of life)."[62] This admission alone is enough to demonstrate that Ayala's defense of general and human evolution is irrelevant when it comes to the debate over ID. Dembski frequently contends that *the fact of evolution* and the claims of ID are fully compatible.[63]

The "Problem" of Natural Selection

The fourth step in Ayala's scientific critique of ID is his explanation of natural selection. While Dembski does not deny the significance of natural selection in driving the evolutionary process, he does view it as severely limited:

> There is no question that Darwin's mutation-selection mechanism constitutes a fruitful idea for biology and one whose fruits have yet to be fully plundered. But Darwinism is more than just this mechanism. Darwinism is the totalizing claim that this mechanism accounts for all the diversity of life. The evidence simply doesn't support this claim.[64]

Dembski and Ayala, therefore, disagree about *the mechanisms of evolution*. This is one aspect of evolution, however, that Ayala admits is legitimately debated among scientists. Even so, he contends that debates regarding the mechanisms of evolution should be restricted to nonteleological mechanisms, whereas ID advocates make no such restrictions. Dembski claims that this is where ID and theistic evolution part ways:

---

62. Dembski, "What Every Theologian Should Know," 227.

63. Again, this does not mean that Dembski personally subscribes to *the fact of evolution*. He writes, "The following problems have proven utterly intractable not only for the mutation-selection mechanism but also for any other undirected natural process proposed to date: the origin of life, the origin of the genetic code, the origin of multicellular life, the origin of sexuality, the scarcity of transitional forms in the fossil record, the biological big bang that occurred in the Cambrian era, the development of complex organ systems and the development of irreducibly complex molecular machines. These are just a few of the more serious difficulties that confront every theory of evolution that posits only undirected natural processes" (Dembski, "What Every Theologian Should Know," 231). Note, however, that Dembski specifically points out that the aforementioned difficulties are difficulties for "undirected natural processes." One could argue this idea is fully consistent with *the fact of evolution* if teleological mechanisms were regarded as appropriate modes of explanation.

64. Dembski, "What Every Theologian Should Know," 230.

> Intelligent design is incompatible with what typically is meant by theistic evolution. Theistic evolution takes the Darwinian picture of the biological world and baptizes it, identifying this picture with the way God created life. When boiled down to its scientific content, however, theistic evolution is no different from atheistic evolution, treating only undirected natural processes in the origin and development of life. Theistic evolution places *theism* and *evolution* in an odd tension. If God purposely created life through Darwinian means, then God's purpose was to make it seem as though life was created without purpose. Within theistic evolution, God is a master of stealth who constantly eludes our best efforts to detect him empirically. Yes, the theistic evolutionist believes that the universe is designed. Yet insofar as there is design in the universe, it is design we recognize strictly through the eyes of faith. Accordingly, the natural world in itself provides no evidence that life is designed. For all we can tell through our natural intellect, our appearance on planet earth is an accident.[65]

Hence the central distinction between theistic evolution and ID is theological. Ayala's theistic evolution seemingly implies that God created the world, but then carefully covered his tracks. This makes God a "stealth designer" according to Dembski.[66] For theists who embrace ID, however, God's design can be observed while studying the natural world.

The fundamental difference between Ayala and Dembski, then, is over the detectability of design. Dembski argues that teleology exists and is discernable in nature. Ayala, on the other hand, argues that Darwin's great accomplishment was to rid teleology from scientific inquiry. After examining Dembski's scientific contributions to ID, however, I think Ayala's argument is grossly exaggerated. Natural selection operating on random variations is certainly a significant mechanism within evolutionary development, but that does not mean that natural selection and random variations are capable of eliminating teleology from biology. To properly assess this greater claim, one needs to consider the philosophical dimensions of the debate over Darwinism, which is the topic of the next chapter.

---

65. Dembski, "What Every Theologian Should Know," 228.
66. Dembski, *Design Revolution*, 7.

5

Defending Intelligent Design Philosophically

DEVELOPING A METHOD FOR detecting design is probably Dembski's most notable contribution to the ID debate. His philosophical contributions, however, are also significant. This is particularly true when considering the problem of dysteleology and suboptimal design. My approach in addressing this problem, therefore, is to utilize Dembksi's work on metaphysics to clarify what type of reality is necessary to make the concept of dysteleology intelligible. Specifically, I will defend Dembski's philosophical critiques of naturalism and materialism to demonstrate the broader claim that non-teleological worldviews are self-referentially incoherent.[1] Regarding the problem with naturalism, Dembski explains,

---

1. I am making a distinction between naturalism and materialism in this chapter, although I will frequently use the terms interchangeably. Using these terms interchangeably seems appropriate since Dembski's earlier theological work on ID typically presents naturalism as an alternative worldview to theism, while his most recent work on metaphysics presents materialism as an alternative to his information-theoretic account of reality. Dembski provides a footnote on his use of terms at the beginning of chapter 3 in *Being as Communion*. He writes, "What I'm calling 'materialism' is usually critiqued under the heading of 'naturalism.' Strictly speaking, naturalism is a doctrine asserting nature's completeness and immunity to any action outside nature (such action would be supernatural). As such, naturalism doesn't stipulate the precise form of nature. But in practice, naturalism tends to devolve into materialism because matter certainly seems an integral part of nature and nothing else seems particularly viable for a hard-nosed understanding of nature. Indeed, what else can there be to nature except matter? Energy, for instance, if not material, promises to become some sort of teleological vital force, which is inconsistent with the sobriety and rigor expected of naturalism. Naturalism is, after all, supposed to keep the world safe from the superstitions of supernaturalism" (Dembski, *Being as Communion*, 17).

For naturalism, epistemology's primary problem is unraveling Einstein's dictum: "The most incomprehensible thing about the world is that it is comprehensible." How is it that we can have any knowledge at all? Within naturalism there is no solution to this riddle.[2]

Without a solution to this riddle, furthermore, naturalism cannot provide epistemic warrant for Ayala's scientific and theological critiques against ID. Traditional theism, on the other hand, does not face the philosophical problem of warrant because it is a teleological worldview. To ground his critiques against ID, therefore, Ayala needs to demonstrate how his nonteleological worldview avoids the self-defeating trap that is confronting naturalism and materialism. I do not think Ayala can do this, which I why I argue that his entire project ironically requires the very teleology he hopes to abandon.

Some Initial Critiques of Naturalism

An examination of Dembski's philosophical works shows that his critiques of naturalism and materialism have remained consistent throughout his scholarly career. Both naturalism and materialism, he argues, assume a nonteleological worldview, implying that any purported examples of teleology—watches, cars, computers, etc.—must ultimately be reduced to nonteleological physical processes. While this implication may seem counterintuitive, one should remember that human artifacts are the products of human brains, and naturalism supports the view that human brains are ultimately the products of unguided and mindless evolutionary developments.[3] Removing teleology from reality, naturalists and materialists are forced to answer a presumably insolvable question regarding the nature of human thinking, namely, what justification does anyone have to suppose that human reasoning is trustworthy? If this question cannot be answered, it suggests that naturalism and materialism are self-defeating worldviews.

---

2. Dembski, *Bridge*, 231–232.

3. Dembski argues, "Naturalism makes intelligence not a basic creative force within nature but an evolutionary byproduct. In particular, humans (the natural objects best known to exhibit intelligence) are not the crown of creation, not the carefully designed outcome of a purposeful creator and certainly not creatures made in the image of a benevolent God. Rather, humans are an accident of natural history" (Dembski, *Design Revolution*, 22).

The details for this argument stem from the notion that all arguments—philosophical, scientific, religious, or otherwise—are constructed by intelligent minds. That is to say, intelligent minds *design* arguments for the purpose of defending certain conclusions. Arguments, then, are a particular type of human artifact. To argue that naturalism and materialism are true is to argue that arguments, like other human artifacts, are ultimately the products of unguided and mindless evolutionary developments. But, if this argument is true, then how can one say that intelligent minds *design* arguments for the purpose of defending certain conclusions? Given naturalism and materialism, the concepts of "intelligent minds" and "design" are hard, if not impossible, to defend. Without these concepts, however, one cannot defend any conclusions, including the conclusions of naturalism or materialism. In other words, carefully constructed arguments cannot exist without design, and naturalism and materialism deny the existence of design. Thus, one cannot construct an argument for naturalism or materialism. Naturalism and materialism both lead to a logically absurd outlook on life.[4]

4. This kind of argument is not unique to Dembski, and has become a fairly common argument among philosophers and Christian apologists over the past several decades. Regarding moral values, C. S. Lewis presents his version of the argument: "In a world of Naturalists [. . .] all moral judgments would be statements about the speaker's feelings, mistaken by him for statements about something else (the real moral quality of actions) which does not exist. Such a doctrine, I have admitted, is not flatly self-contradictory" (Lewis, *Miracles*, 57). Alvin Plantinga develops the argument as an evolutionary argument against naturalism (EAAN). He writes, "if *naturalism* is true, there is no God, and hence no God (or anyone else) overseeing our development and orchestrating the course of our evolution. And this leads directly to the question whether it is at all likely that our cognitive faculties, given naturalism and given their evolutionary origin, would have developed in such a way as to be reliable, to furnish us with mostly true beliefs" (Plantinga, "Evolutionary Argument against Naturalism," 3).

Plantinga's argument is further expressed in Charles Darwin's famous doubt, "With me the horrid doubt always arises whether the convictions of man's mind, which has been developed from the mind of lower animals, are of any value or at all trustworthy. Would anyone trust in the convictions of a monkey's mind, if there are any convictions in such a mind?" (Darwin, "Letter to William Graham," 285). Or consider Patricia Churchland's often cited passage, "Boiled down to essentials, a nervous system enables the organism to succeed in the four F's: feeding, fleeing, fighting and reproducing. The principle chore of nervous systems is to get the body parts where they should be in order that the organism may survive . . . . Improvements in sensorimotor control confer an evolutionary advantage: a fancier style of representing is advantageous *so long as it is geared to the organism's way of life and enhances the organism's chances of survival*. Truth, whatever that is, definitely takes the hindmost" (Churchland, "Epistemology," 548). Thomas Nagel agrees with Plantinga, arguing that, "Evolutionary naturalism implies that we shouldn't take any of our convictions seriously, including the scientific world picture on which

The aforementioned argument is a crude, but pointed, introduction to Dembski's fundamental critique against naturalism and materialism. If his critique is correct, then Ayala's arguments against ID cannot be grounded in naturalism or materialism. Of course, Ayala will likely find this point irrelevant since he rejects materialism and naturalism.[5] He does not, however, provide a clear nonteleological theistic alternative.[6] He also explicitly rejects a teleological account of reality, which arguably makes his nebulous description of theism susceptible to the same epistemological problems facing naturalism and materialism.

To fully appreciate the epistemological problems stated above, it is useful to examine how the core of Dembski's argument against naturalism and materialism has developed over time. In Dembski's early work on ID, he frequently constructed philosophical, theological, and methodological arguments against naturalism, denouncing it as one of the greatest idols in our culture. He explains,

> Those who are blind to God's action in the world have one overriding satisfaction: That this world belongs to them and to them alone. Call those who are blind to God's action in the world "naturalists," and call the view that nature is self-contained "naturalism." For the naturalist God plays no role in the world. Religious believers are apt to think that a world without God is a terribly sad place in which no one given the choice would want to live. But to the naturalist it is precisely the presence of God in the world that threatens to undo it.[7]

Dembski frequently held that debates about naturalism went beyond science. His colleague, Phillip Johnson, likewise emphasized this point—arguing that naturalism was replacing Christian theism as the dominant

---

evolutionary naturalism itself depends" (Nagel, *Mind & Cosmos*, 28). In the body of this chapter, I also refer to other thinkers who articulate similar arguments pertaining to the problem against naturalism.

5. As mentioned in chapter 2, Ayala rejects metaphysical naturalism but embraces methodological naturalism, claiming that, "a scientific view of the world is hopelessly incomplete. Matters of value and meaning are outside science's scope" (Ayala, *Darwin and Intelligent Design*, 102).

6. Furthermore, his fundamental solution to the problem of dysteleology and suboptimal design is to reduce the modes of causation in nature to merely chance and necessity. See chapter 3.

7. Dembski, *Bridge*, 99.

religious voice in the culture. Johnson furthermore described naturalism as a *metaphysical* doctrine, stating,

> What is ultimately real is nature, which consists of the fundamental particles that make up what we call matter and energy, together with the natural laws that govern how those particles behave. Nature itself is ultimately all there is, at least as far as we are concerned. To put it another way, nature is a permanently closed system of material causes and effects that can never be influenced by anything outside of itself—by God, for example. To speak of something as "supernatural" is therefore to imply that it is imaginary, and belief in powerful imaginary entities is known as superstition.[8]

This religion, according to Johnson, will not grant the existence of supernatural entities because, in principle, supernatural entities are antithetical to naturalism. Naturalism further implies that teleological entities are supernatural, since all particles of reality are governed by nonteleological natural laws. Thus naturalism cannot support ID, because naturalism is a nonteleological worldview.

Like Johnson's work, Dembski's early writings also addressed the metaphysical and religious dimensions of the debate over Darwinism and ID. As mentioned in chapter 1, this engagement often confused critics of ID, especially when Dembski (and other ID advocates) contributed to the creation-evolution controversy. One can therefore understand why many critics have pointed to such participation as evidence for the claim that ID is merely repackaged creationism.[9]

Dembski's contribution to the debates over creation and evolution, however, primarily focused on worldview questions. He explains,

> We are dealing here with something more than a straightforward determination of scientific facts or confirmation of scientific theories. Rather we are dealing with competing worldviews and incompatible metaphysical systems. In the creation-evolution controversy we are dealing with a naturalistic metaphysic that shapes and controls what theories of biological origins are permitted on the playing field in advance of any discussion or weighing of evidence. This metaphysic is so pervasive and powerful that it

---

8. Johnson, *Reason in the Balance*, 37–38.

9. This thesis is highlighted in edited volumes such as Petto and Godfrey, *Scientists Confront Intelligent Design*; Pennock, *Intelligent Design Creationism*; Comfort, *Panda's Black Box*.

not only rules alternative views out of court, but it cannot even permit itself to be criticized.[10]

Dembski's point is that ID faces obstacles, not because of the physical evidence, but because the "scientific outlook" on nature undermines the teleological notions of creation. In order for ID to gain credibility, therefore, many ID advocates sought to challenge the notion that nature is self-contained and self-driven. Again, Dembski writes,

> Turn on the television to watch a nature program and you will be regaled with all the wonderful things nature does. Nature is responsible for the giraffe's neck, the eagle's talons and the angler fish's lure. Nature gives us rain forests, roses and rutabagas. Nature feeds, clothes and entertains us. Nature spans everything from quarks to galaxy clusters. Most significant, we are part of nature. With nature fulfilling so many vital roles, it's fair to ask, What is nature? Definitions abound. Nature is the material or physical world. Nature is the biophysical universe. Nature is the natural order. Nature is the realm of space, time and energy. Nature is that part of reality described by natural laws. Nature is what scientists study—the domain of science.[11]

He continues,

> Each of these definitions is right as far as it goes. Implicit in these definitions, however, is a telling omission. In no instance do we find nature identified with creation. To be sure, in common parlance we often merge the two, referring to nature and creation interchangeably. But creation is always a divine act, whereas nature is a self-contained entity independent of God. God is irrelevant to nature. Nature treats the world as though it were self-sufficient and not in need of a creator. Creation requires a creator, but nature requires no creator. A creator might exist, but one need not exist for the world to be nature. Nature is what the world would be if there were no God.[12]

These two paragraphs elucidate Dembski's distinction between *nature* and *creation*, asserting that *creation* is a more appropriate term than *nature* when describing the observable world. If his assertion is correct, then

---

10. Dembski, *Bridge*, 115.
11. Dembski, *Bridge*, 97.
12. Dembski, *Bridge*, 97–98.

presumably God's interaction with the world might be empirically detectable.[13] If the observable world is simply *nature*, however, then God either does not exist or is "marvelously adept at covering his tracks and giving no evidence that he ever interacted with the world."[14] Dembski thus maintains that a theist who describes the observable world naturalistically is, practically speaking, no different than an atheist.[15]

After clarifying the distinction between nature and creation, Dembski constructs arguments against naturalism and for a Christian doctrine of creation. In doing so, he is not arguing for a specific doctrine of creation. Rather, he is claiming that naturalism and Christianity "provide radically different perspectives on the act of creation."[16] Specifically, he calls naturalism a *matter-first* worldview, whereas theism is a *mind-first* worldview. He explains,

> The naturalist's world is not a mind-first world. Intelligent agency is neither sui generis nor basic.... It is important to distinguish the naturalist's understanding of causation from the theist's. Within theism God is the ultimate reality. Consequently whenever God acts, there can be nothing outside of God that compels God's action. God is not a billiard ball that must move when another billiard ball strikes it. God's actions are free, and though he responds to his creation, he does not do so out of necessity. Within theism, therefore, divine action is not reducible to some more basic mode of causation. . . . Now consider naturalism. Within naturalism nature is the ultimate reality. Consequently whenever something happens in nature, there can be nothing outside of nature that shares responsibility for what happened.[17]

These two worldviews thus promote two competing notions of causation within the observable world. Theism argues that God is the ultimate reality; naturalism argues that nature is the ultimate reality. Naturalism contends

---

13. Dembski, *Bridge*, 104.

14. Dembski, *Bridge*, 104. This is apparently the position of Ayala. God exists, but has chosen not to make his existence evident in the natural world.

15. Dembski, *Bridge*, 110. Again, Ayala seems to fit this description. This does not mean, of course, that Ayala should be regarded as an atheist. One can certainly argue that metaphysical precision and accuracy is not a prerequisite for an authentic faith. Dembski's point is that a nonteleological conception of theism seems virtually indistinguishable from naturalism.

16. Dembski, *Bridge*, 212.

17. Dembski, *Bridge*, 214.

that nature governs all events according to necessity or chance, whereas theism opens the door for God to govern events according to his free actions and choices. These two worldviews, therefore, are fundamentally in conflict according to Dembski.

Dembski further notes that the distinction between a matter-first and mind-first worldview is significant when addressing the mystery of human agency. How can a matter-first worldview give rise to intelligent human agency? Dembski argues that this question cannot be answered:

> [For the naturalist], intelligent agency is . . . in no sense prior to or independent of nature. Intelligent agency is neither sui generis nor basic. Intelligent agency is a derivative mode of causation that depends on underlying naturalistic—and therefore unintelligent—causes. Human agency in particular supervenes on underlying natural processes, which in turn are usually identified with brain function.[18]

In other words, the question cannot be answered because intelligent human agency cannot be reduced to underlying natural processes. In recent years, the depth of this problem has only seemed to increase. David Chalmers, for example, is famous for introducing he calls the hard problem of consciousness.[19] Roughly stated, the hard problem of consciousness seeks to understand how mass, time, and space give rise to a first-person conscious experience. Chalmers maintains that there are no current plausible answers to this question, and therefore one must be willing to embrace

---

18. Dembski, *Bridge*, 214.

19. When discussing the hard problem of consciousness, Chalmers distinguishes it from the "easy" problems. The easy problems, according to Chalmers, are problems that can be solved using the standard methods of cognitive science. The hard problem of consciousness, by contrast, is the problem of experience. Chalmers writes, "When we think and perceive, there is a whir of information processing, but there is also a subjective aspect. As Nagel (1974) has put it, there is *something it is like* to be a conscious organism. This subjective aspect is experience. When we see, for example, we *experience* visual sensations: the felt quality of redness, the experience of dark and light, the quality of depth in a visual field. . . . It is undeniable that some organisms are subjects of experience, but the question of why it is that these systems are subjects of experience is perplexing. Why is it that when our cognitive systems engage in visual and auditory information processing, we have visual or auditory experience: the quality of deep blue, the sensation of middle C? How can we explain why there is something it is like to entertain a mental image or to experience an emotion? It is widely agreed that experience arises from a physical basis, but we have no good explanation of why and how it so arises. Why should a physical processing give rise to a rich inner life at all? It seems objectively unreasonable that it should, and yet it does" (Chalmers, *Character of Consciousness*, 5).

counterintuitive ideas. The counterintuitive idea put forth by Chalmers is known as panpsychism—the idea that consciousness is just as fundamental as mass, time, and space.[20] While Chalmers admits that his view is strange, he maintains that it is just as plausible as the alternative counterintuitive idea, namely, that consciousness is an illusion.[21]

Chalmers and his hard problem of consciousness will be explored more fully in chapter 6. I briefly mention it here to highlight that Dembski is not alone in recognizing the problem naturalism has in accounting for human agency and consciousness. Chalmers embraces the difficulty and argues that consciousness must be a fundamental aspect of reality. Dembski, likewise, embraces the difficulty but argues that consciousness is *the fundamental aspect of reality*, and consequently mass, time, and space are contingent derivatives.

Given a matter-first worldview, Dembski reasons that human agency is an illusion. This is problematic when one considers that human agency produces every thought, argument, judgment, and emotion experienced by a human subject. If human agency is an illusion, then how can one ground the arguments that presumably lead one to conclude that human agency is an illusion? Naturalism, as mentioned in the introduction of this chapter, faces the epistemological problem of being self-referentially incoherent, because naturalism implies that human agency is an illusion.

Of course, other philosophers and apologists have long recognized and highlighted the self-defeating aspects of naturalism. C.S. Lewis, for example, elegantly captures the problem in the following paragraphs:

> All possible knowledge . . . depends on the validity of reasoning. If the feeling of certainty which we express by words like *must be* and

---

20. Chalmers explains, "the view can be seen as a sort of neutral monism: there are underlying neutral properties X (the protophenomenal properties), such that the X properties are simultaneously responsible for constituting the physical domain (by their relations) and the phenomenal domain (by their collective intrinsic nature). In its phenomenal form, the view can be seen as a sort of idealism, such that mental properties constitute physical properties, although these need not be mental properties in the mind of an observer, and they may need to be supplemented by causal and spatiotemporal properties in addition. One could also characterize this form of view as a sort of panpsychism, with phenomenal properties ubiquitous at the fundamental level" (Chalmers, *Character of Consciousness*, 134).

21. Daniel Dennett defends this second counterintuitive idea. He argues, "While there are still thinkers who gamely hold out for consciousness being some one genuine precious thing (like love, like gold), a thing that is just 'obvious' and very, very special, the suspicion is growing that this is an illusion" (Dennett, *Consciousness Explained*, 23).

therefore and *since* is a real perception of how things outside our own minds really "must" be, well and good. But if this certainty is merely a feeling *in* our own minds and not a genuine insight into realities beyond them—if it merely represents the way our minds happen to work—then we can have no knowledge. Unless human reasoning is valid no science can be true.[22]

He continues,

It follows that no account of the universe can be true unless that account leaves it possible for our thinking to be a real insight. A theory which explained everything else in the whole universe but which made it impossible to believe that our thinking was valid, would be utterly out of court. For that theory would itself have been reached by thinking, and if thinking is not valid that theory would, of course, be itself demolished. It would have destroyed its own credentials. It would be an argument which proved that no argument was—a proof that there are no such things as proofs—which is nonsense.[23]

By describing naturalism as a theory that explains "everything else in the whole universe but which made it impossible to believe that our thinking was valid," Lewis cleverly highlights the logical incoherence of naturalism.

Alvin Plantinga, likewise, has published extensively on what he calls the evolutionary argument against naturalism (EAAN).[24] He explains,

---

22. Lewis, *Miracles*, 21.

23. Lewis, *Miracles*, 21–22.

24. For his most recent example, see Plantinga, *Where the Conflict Really Lies*. Plantinga's warrant series further provides an exhaustive treatment of various epistemological problems with nonteleological approaches knowledge, and concludes by contending that a belief B, " has warrant for you if and only if (1) the cognitive faculties involved in the production of B are functioning properly . . . (2) your cognitive environment is sufficiently similar to the one for which your cognitive faculties are designed; (3) the triple of the design plan governing the production of the belief in question involves, as purpose or function, the production of true beliefs (and the same goes for elements of the design plan governing the production of input beliefs to the system in question); and (4) the design plan is a good one: that is, there is a high statistical or objective probability that a belief produced in accordance with the relevant segament of the design plan in that sort of environment is true. Under these conditions, furthermore, the degree of warrant is given by some monotonically increasing function of the strength of S's belief that B. This account of warrant, therefore, depends essentially upon the notion of proper function" (Plantinga, *Warrant and Proper Function*, 194). See also Plantinga, *Warrant: The Current Debate*; *Warranted Christian Belief*.

> The basic idea of my argument could be put ... as follows. First, the probability of our cognitive faculties being reliable, given naturalism and evolution, is low. (To put it a bit inaccurately but suggestively, if naturalism and evolution were both true, our cognitive faculties would very likely not be reliable.) But then according to the second premise of my argument, if I believe both naturalism and evolution, I have a *defeater* for my intuitive assumption that my cognitive faculties are reliable. If I have a defeater for *that* belief, however, then I have a defeater for *any* belief I take to be produced by my cognitive faculties. That means that I have a defeater for my belief that naturalism and evolution are true. So my belief that naturalism and evolution are true gives me a defeater for that very belief; that belief shoots itself in the foot and is self-referentially incoherent; therefore I cannot rationally accept it. And if one can't accept both naturalism and evolution, that pillar of current science, then there is serious conflict between naturalism and science.[25]

Plantinga's EAAN has certainly sparked controversy over the past few decades, but the argument continues to influence both theistic and non-theistic philosophers.[26] Thomas Nagel, for example, agrees with the central premise of Plantinga's argument, affirming that, "the application of evolutionary theory to the understanding of our own cognitive capacities should undermine, though it need not completely destroy, our confidence in them."[27] Nagel agues this because the mechanisms of belief formation, given naturalism, are not aimed at constructing true theoretical accounts of the world.[28] Thus, we have no reason to trust any of our beliefs.

In addition to EAAN, other related criticisms of naturalism continue to develop. Victor Reppert constructs the following argument:[29]

---

25. Plantinga, *Where the Conflict Really Lies*, 314. Plantinga abbreviates this argument as: "P(R/N&E) is low. 'R' is the proposition that our cognitive faculties are reliable, 'N' is naturalism, and 'E' is the proposition that we and our cognitive faculties have come to be in the way proposed by the contemporary scientific theory of evolution. 'P(. . . /____)' is shorthand for 'the probability of ... given ____'" (Plantinga, *Where the Conflict Really Lies*, 317).

26. For an introduction to the common objections raised against EAAN, see Beilby, *Naturalism Defeated?*

27. Nagel, *Mind & Cosmos*, 27.

28. Nagel, *Mind & Cosmos*, 27.

29. Reppert, "Argument from Reason," 347.

1. Either at least some of the fundamental causes of the universe are more like a mind than anything else, or they are not.
2. If they are not, then it is either impossible or extremely improbable that reason should emerge.
3. All things being equal, worldviews that render it impossible or extremely improbable that reason should emerge should be rejected in favor of worldviews according to which it is not impossible and not improbable that reason should emerge.
4. Therefore, we have good reason to reject all worldviews that reject the claim that the fundamental causes of the universe are more like a mind than anything else.

Reppert has naturalism and materialism in mind when he describes any worldview that rejects "the claim that the fundamental causes of the universe are more like a mind than anything else." William Hasker, similarly, critiques physicalism as follows:

> Given the physicalist assumption, *the occurrence and content of conscious mental states such as belief and desire are irrelevant to behavior and are not subject to selection pressures.* On this assumption, *natural selection gives us no reason to assume that the experiential content of mental states corresponds in any way whatever to objective reality.* And since on the physicalist scenario Darwinist epistemology is the *only* available explanation for the reliability of our epistemic faculties, the conclusion to be drawn is that physicalism not only *has not given* any explanation for such reliability, but it *is in principle unable to give* any such explanation. And that, it seems to me, is about as devastating an objection to physicalism as anyone could hope to find.[30]

Hasker's objection to physicalism provides a more aggressive form of the argument against naturalism. Whereas Plantinga, Nagel, and Reppert leave room for the unlikely chance that naturalism might produce reliable epistemic faculties, Hasker contends that such a scenario cannot happen *in principle*. On Hasker's account of the argument, naturalism is hopelessly self-defeating.

Again, Dembski has many allies when it comes to his general argument against naturalism. His particular focus as an ID advocate, however,

---

30. Hasker, *Emergent Self*, 79. While Hasker uses the word "physicalism" rather than "naturalism," there is practically no difference in the meaning of these two terms.

introduces additional critiques against Darwinian naturalism. According to Dembski, Darwinism is a naturalistic worldview that defends of three distinct notions. First, Darwinism defends its *physical content*, which refers to the notion of common descent within biology. Second, Darwinism defends its *theoretical content*, which refers to the mutation-selection mechanism as the sole driving force of the evolutionary process. Last, Darwinism defends its *regulative principles* articulated by *methodological naturalism* (MN).[31]

By articulating Darwinism as an overarching worldview with these three aspects, Dembski brings further clarity to his understanding of the debate over ID. Intelligent Design, for Dembski, does not necessarily deny the physical content of Darwinism, but it does reject Darwinism's theoretical content and its regulative principles.[32] Clarifying this issue suggests that the Darwinism/ID debate is more philosophical than scientific. When it comes to Darwinism's theoretical content, there are no scientific arguments to demonstrate that chance mutations and natural selection are the *only* driving forces of evolution. Furthermore, empirical investigations cannot determine that nonteleological mechanisms are the *only* viable alternatives to Darwinism's theoretical content. As for MN—the regulative principles of Darwinism—this debate is purely philosophical.

At this point, then, we can further clarify that the chief differences between Dembski and Ayala lie in their different perspectives concerning the theoretical content and regulative principles of Darwinism. Dembski explains,

> Theistic evolutionists [like Ayala] think Darwin got nature right and then adapt their theology to suit Darwinian science. Proponents of intelligent design, by contrast, ask the logically prior question whether Darwin did in fact get nature right. Indeed, why should we think that natural forces, apart from intelligent guidance, have the power to create biological information?[33]

---

31. For a full discussion on these ideas, see Dembski, "Task of Apologetics," 36.

32. In chapter 2, Ayala makes distinctions between the fact of evolution, the history of evolution, and the mechanism of evolution. As argued earlier, ID is consistent with the fact and history of evolution, even though many ID advocates critique both.

33. Dembski and Marks, "Life's Conservation Law," 365. Dembski further explains, "Because God is intimately involved with the world moment by moment, there is no question that God interacts with the world. This is a tenet of our faith that brooks no controversy. Controversy arises, however, once we ask whether God's interaction with the world is *empirically detectable*. It is one thing as a matter of faith to hold that God exists, interacts with and sovereignly rules the world. Alternatively, it may be argued on philosophical grounds that the world and its laws are not self-explanatory and therefore

Note that Dembski is not debating Darwin's scientific observations, but rather the naturalistic implications that theistic evolutionists draw from Darwin's observations. Such implications are apparent in Ayala's work, most noticeably in his central claim that Darwin's great accomplishment was to demonstrate how life could arise without teleology. If Ayala is correct in this claim, then Darwin's great accomplishment was more about philosophy than science.

Recognizing the philosophical nature of this alleged accomplishment, furthermore, helps one articulate the worldview implications of Darwin. Ayala's claim is that Darwin demonstrates a nonteleological outlook on nature; therefore, a Darwinian worldview must be nonteleological. What, then, makes this worldview different than naturalism? Dembski argues that there is no difference, and consequently he understands why atheists are drawn to Darwinianism. He does not understand, however, why professing theists would adopt Darwinism. Theistic evolutionists seemingly join hands with atheists by "proclaiming that purposeful design in biology is *scientifically undetectable*."[34] Ayala takes this even further by proclaiming that teleology is not only undetectable, but also absent from nature.

One might think, therefore, that Ayala is a naturalist. Ayala rejects this charge, claiming that he embraces methodological (rather than metaphysical) naturalism. Naturalism, he contends, should only apply within the domain of science. Outside of that domain, one can talk freely about purpose, morality, and even spiritual realities. From Ayala's perspective, many controversies in the religion and science dialogue would be avoided if theologians and scientists would merely distinguish science from other lines of intellectual inquiry. Both religious and non-religious participants of the science versus religion debate, however, presumably fail to recognize such simple distinctions. Ayala explains,

> The well-known evolutionist Richard Dawkins explicitly denies design, purpose, and values: "the universe that we observe has precisely the properties we should expect if there is, at bottom, no design, no purpose, no evil and no good, nothing but blind, pitiless indifference." It is ironic that [authors like Dawkins] are, in fact, endorsing the beliefs of ID proponents who argue that

---

point to a transcendent source. But it is another matter entirely to assert that the empirical evidence supports God's interaction with the world, rendering God's interaction empirically detectable" (Dembski, "What Every Theologian Should Know," 222).

34. Dembski and Marks, "Life's Conservation Law," 365.

science is inherently materialistic and share the ID conceit that science makes assertions about values, meaning, and purpose.[35]

According to Ayala, Dawkins and ID advocates both embrace a fallacious version of scientism, which assumes that science provides the only source of knowledge about reality. Ayala rejects this notion, and wants to affirm that one can discover values, meaning, and purpose outside of scientific investigation.

Ayala furthermore views his rejection of scientism as stemming from his affirmation of MN as the regulatory principle of science.[36] Methodological naturalism, he contends, permits one to embrace the best aspects of science, while rejecting the notion that science tells us everything about the human experience. Ayala explains,

> A scientific view of the world is hopelessly incomplete. There are matters of value and meaning that are outside science's scope. Even when we have a satisfying scientific understanding of a natural object or process, we are still missing matters that may well be thought by many to be of equal or greater import.[37]

Ayala is right to mention the limitations of science, and to recognize that a coherent worldview must leave room for disciplines like metaphysics, logic, ethics, aesthetics, mathematics, religion, and other lines of inquiry. If fact, contra Ayala, Dembski and other ID advocates frequently argue for the limitations of science.[38] Thus what separates Dembski from Ayala on this point, is that each thinker has a different perspective on how science re-

---

35. Ayala, *Darwin and Intelligent Design*, 101–2.

36. Ayala also mentions three traits that distinguish science from all other forms of knowledge. First, science is different than common sense because science is concerned with formulating general laws and theories that manifest patterns of relations between very different kinds of phenomena. Second, science seeks to formulate explanations for natural phenomena by identifying the conditions that account for their occurrence. At this point, science is within the same classification as mathematics, philosophy, and theology. The third distinction is what makes it different, namely, empirical falsification. Falsification is the proper demarcation that sets science apart from other forms of knowledge, an idea that Karl Popper calls the criterion of demarcation. He also mentions four other ideas: (1) science must be internally consistent, (2) science must have explanatory value, (3) a scientific finding must be consistent with preexisting scientific knowledge, and (4) a scientific idea must be tested empirically (Ayala, "From Paley to Darwin," 56–57). For Popper on the criterion of demarcation, see Popper, *Two Fundamental Problems*, 10–11.

37. Ayala, "From Paley to Darwin," 57–58.

38. For example, see Moreland, *Scientism and Secularism*.

lates to other domains of knowledge. Ayala seems to think that the various domains have little or no relationship with each other, whereas Dembski allows for more continuity between the disciplines.

To appreciate why this continuity matters to Dembski, we might consider some of his early critiques of MN. Dembski argues that MN is reasonable only if metaphysical naturalism is true. He begins this argument by first grouping naturalism into four categories—antiteleological naturalism (ATN), methodological naturalism (MN), antisupernaturalistic naturalism (ASN), and pragmatic naturalism (PN). Dembski defines ATN as philosophical or metaphysical naturalism, where nature is self-contained and operates solely according to blind physical processes.[39] He explains,

> Antiteleological naturalism is the predominant form of naturalism—it's what's usually meant by the term *naturalism*. Antiteleological naturalism takes nature to be all there is and views nature, at the nuts-and-bolts level, as operating purely by blind natural causes. These are causes characterized by chance and necessity and ruled by unbroken natural laws.[40]

This version of naturalism, for Dembski, implies that there is no objective meaning, purpose, or values in the real world. Such an implication is a metaphysical, but it also spills over into other domains of knowledge. An ethicist, for example, could not consistently embrace ATN while also arguing for, say, John Rawls's egalitarian approach to social justice.[41] This is because ATN denies the existence of objective meaning, purpose, or values—meaning that Rawls's theory of justice is neither true nor false. It seems obvious, then, that our metaphysical commitments can either support or undermine our conclusions about moral objectivism in the domain of ethics. Thus, we cannot completely separate the various domains of knowledge.

In Dembski's critique of MN, he further illustrates the relationships between different domains of knowledge. As mentioned above, Ayala argues that MN represents the scientific way of knowing, but not the only way of knowing. He thus wants to separate different domains of

---

39. In this distinction, Dembski also includes epistemological naturalism, reductive naturalism, scientific naturalism, scientific materialism, materialism, and physicalism (Dembski, *Design Revolution*, 169, 171–72).

40. Dembski, *Design Revolution*, 169.

41. I am not arguing here that an ethicist would never attempt to do such a thing; rather, I am simply arguing that ethicists who do so are arguing inconsistently.

knowledge into different spheres. Dembski attempts to further articulate Ayala's piont, stating,

> Methodological naturalism ... is willing to grant that there may be more to reality than chance and necessity. Methodological naturalism doesn't care what you believe deep down. Yet for the sake of science, methodological naturalism insists that scientists pretend as though antiteleological naturalism is true. Nancey Murphy has called this view *methodological atheism*. The idea here is that science is a method for investigating nature and that to understand nature scientists must only invoke "natural processes." In this context the term "natural processes" means processes operating entirely according to unbroken natural laws and characterized by chance and necessity.[42]

In other words, MN is not supposed to reject teleology as a metaphysical belief. It merely proposes that topics related to teleology are not scientific in nature.

Dembski challenges this principle, claiming that it rules out the possibility of ID before an honest investigation of the relevant data. Furthermore, he contends that advocates of MN are unwilling to allow other plausible methods into scientific discourse:

> If methodological naturalism were merely a working hypothesis, maintained because it supposedly has served science well in the past, that would be one thing. As a working hypothesis, it would be optional, and scientists who found the hypothesis no longer helpful would be free to discard it. But methodological naturalism isn't saying that we have yet to encounter empirical evidence of design in nature but we should stay open to it in case it comes along. Rather, methodological naturalism insists that one is most logical, most scientific, if one pretends such an empirical possibility is logically impossible. Instead of holding methodological naturalism as a working hypothesis, methodological naturalists hold it as a dogma.[43]

Put succinctly, MN is not based upon evidence; rather, it is a philosophical assumption that unnecessarily eliminates teleological explanations from science. Again, Dembski explains, "The rule that science should refuse teleology seems ... less a requirement of science as such than a

---

42. Dembski, *Design Revolution*, 170.
43. Dembski, *Design Revolution*, 171.

logical consequence of [naturalism]: if [naturalism] is true, then no fundamental or real teleology can exist in nature for science to study; instead, any teleology or intelligence in nature must result from underlying non-teleological processes."[44] If one thought it were possible for life to exhibit design, however, then Dembski submits that one should adopt a regulatory principle that makes it possible to detect design in biology. Methodological Naturalism does not make design detection possible, which suggests that it can only be reasonable if ATN is true.

In addition to ATN and MN, Dembski's articulation of ASN and PN are also significant. Antisupernaturalist Naturalism maintains that supernatural activities cannot be detected in the natural world. This position is distinct from ATN, because detecting design is not the same thing as detecting supernatural activities. Explaining such nuances, Dembski writes,

> Antisupernaturalist naturalism, like Christian theism, leaves nature open to real teleology and so opens the door to intelligent design as a scientific enterprise. In contrast, antiteleological and methodological naturalism completely rule out intelligent design as a scientific project: intelligent design is a nonstarter if one adopts either of these views. Nevertheless, because antisupernaturalist naturalism is so much friendlier to intelligent design, one runs the risk of overlooking just how metaphysically uneasy is the fit between intelligent design and antisupernaturalist naturalism. The problem is that the whole concept of design implies giving something a capacity it did not possess before. As Aristotle put it, the art of ship building is not in the wood; it takes a designer to arrange the wood to make the ship. Design arranges preexisting materials and thereby confers on them something they did not previously possess. But within antisupernaturalist naturalism, there is no bestowing of any gift on nature. Naturalism, whether antisupernaturalist or antiteleological, views nature as the ultimate reality and one that is complete in itself.[45]

The theological differences between ATN and ASN are minor, from Dembski's perspective; nevertheless, ASN leaves room for discussions about teleology and intelligence within nature.

---

44. Dembski, *Being as Communion*, 49–50. Note that this quote does not come from Dembski's early critiques of naturalism, and also note that I replaced the word "materialism" with "naturalism."

45. Dembski, *Design Revolution*, 176.

Dembski's last version of naturalism is PN, which states that the goal of science is simply to understand nature. This approach is distinct from MN because it is not concerned with removing teleological explanations from science, so long as such explanations are insightful. Dembski explains,

> Pragmatic naturalism wants simply to understand nature and doesn't care what entities are invoked to facilitate that understanding, so long as they prove conceptually fruitful. The philosopher Willard Quine was a pragmatic naturalist (as was Ludwig Wittgenstein). Accordingly, Quine was able to entertain the following possibility: "If I saw indirect explanatory benefit in positing sensibilia, possibilia, spirits, a Creator, I would joyfully accord them scientific status too, on par with such avowedly scientific posits as quarks and black holes." Quine's pragmatic naturalism clearly places no restrain on the intelligent design.[46]

Thus, Dembski reasons that if PN were the operating principle of scientific investigation, then there would be no philosophical conflict between ID and the scientific community.

Recent Critiques of Materialism

Similar to Dembski's early critiques of naturalism are his more recent critiques of materialism.[47] In *Being as Communion*, Dembski argues against materialism in favor of an information-theoretic account of reality. Materialism suggests that all information and perceived teleology is reduced to material substances and causes. Particles, in other words, are the fundamental stuff of reality. Dembski notes that this perspective on reality undermines the notions of design, information, and even basic intelligibility:

> Because matter is all that exists within materialism, any design will just be one item of matter causing a change in another item of matter. And since matter at root is nonteleological, any teleology

---

46. Dembski, *Design Revolution*, 177.

47. Dembski explains his use of the word *materialism* over *naturalism* in his later works: "What I'm calling 'materialism' is usually critiqued under the heading of 'naturalism.' Strictly speaking, naturalism is a doctrine asserting nature's completeness and immunity to any action outside nature (such action would be supernatural). As such, naturalism doesn't stipulate the precise form of nature. But in practice, naturalism tends to devolve into materialism because matter certainly seems an integral part of nature and nothing else seems particularly viable for a hard-nosed understanding of nature. Indeed, what else can there be to nature except matter?" (Dembski, *Being as Communion*, 17).

associated with such design is, in the end, merely a byproduct of underlying nonteleological material processes. In this way, materialism destroys any fundamental or real teleology in nature.[48]

This leads to the absurd conclusion that every example of design—including books, ships, computers, and other examples of human design—are actually not designed. Instead, all of these examples are ultimately reduced to nonteleological explanations.[49]

Dembski expresses his argument for this conclusion when he rhetorically asks, "If humans are the product of natural selection (conceived nonteleologically), would not ships themselves be an indirect product of natural selection?"[50] Materialism, he argues, forces one to explain every object in terms of blind physical forces. If this claim is correct, then Dembski notes that there is a significant conflict between materialism and epistemology. He explains, "How can knowing subjects composed only of matter know that they are only composed of matter? Matter, it would seem, has no intrinsic capacity to produce agents that think, much less that can form representations about the world, much less that can know that these representations are true."[51] The problem Dembski is raising here is similar to the epistemological problem he raised against naturalism. Materialists claim that the mental states of conscious human knowers supervene on material brain states. This means that every conscious thought, every philosophical

---

48. Dembski, *Being as Communion*, 57.

49. Dembski reiterates this point when he writes, "Humans have designed all sorts of engineering marvels, everything from Cray supercomputers to Gothic cathedrals. But that means, we are to believe . . . that a blind evolutionary process cobbled together human neuroanatomy, which in turn gave rise to human consciousness, which in turn produces artifacts like supercomputers, which in turn are not cobbled together at all but instead carefully designed. Out pop purpose, intelligence, and design from a process that started with no purpose, intelligence, or design. This is magic" (Dembski, "What Intelligent Design is Not," 21).

50. Dembski, *Being as Communion*, 55–56. Ayala writes, "Inanimate objects and processes (other than those created by humans) are not teleological because they are not directed toward specific ends, they do not exist to serve certain purposes" (Ayala, "Chance and Necessity," 240). Contra Ayala, Dembski asks, "Where does design or intelligent causation fit within this dialectic between chance and necessity? It doesn't. At best design becomes a byproduct of chance and necessity. If, for instance, the Darwinian mechanism of random variation and natural selection accounts for the emergence of human beings, then human intelligence (with all its design capabilities) is merely a complex behavioral capacity that sits atop blind material processes" (Dembski, *Design Revolution*, 80).

51. Dembski, *Being as Communion*, 7.

argument, and every scientific insight is traced back to unconscious synaptic firings in the brain.⁵² Dembski continues,

> Because materialism gives primacy to matter, it downgrades the role of intelligence in nature, conceiving of nature in purely material terms, thus making intelligence a byproduct of material nature rather than its source and purpose. Materialism sees matter as fundamentally non-intelligent, and it thus needs to constitute intelligence out of matter.⁵³

Materialism, like naturalism, makes it difficult to justify the position that our cognitive faculties are generally reliable guides to truth. Thus, materialism is likewise a self-defeating worldview that fundamentally undermines scientific investigation.

The aforementioned critique of materialism, like Dembski's critiques of Darwinism and naturalism, should not lead to the conclusion that unguided natural processes are wholly irrelevant. Dembski's argument against materialism is simply suggesting that unguided natural processes cannot be fundamental to reality. This does not discount the possibility that some surface-level events will be best explained by mindless natural activities. For example, one might reasonably explain the motion of planets, stars, and galaxies in terms of unguided physical forces. Dembski does not dispute such explanations. But when it comes to events like the origin of life, consciousness, language, or human intentions, he contends that materialistic explanations are insufficient and often self-referentially incoherent.⁵⁴

Materialism furthermore leads to an ethical problem, because it cannot ground moral knowledge by implication. Moral values are the product of conscious judgments, and materialism undermines the notion of conscious judgments. Dembski explains,

> On materialist grounds, neither praise nor blame makes any sense. A ball rolls down an inclined plane (deterministically) and smashes a teacup; a coin is flipped and by landing heads (probabilistically) causes a teacup to fall and smash. No one blames the ball or

---

52. For more information on the philosophical issues related to consciousness, see Searle, *Mystery of Consciousness*; Chalmers, *Character of Consciousness*; Dennett, *Consciousness Explained*; Nagel, *Mind & Cosmos*.

53. Dembski, *Being as Communion*, 48. Elsewhere, Dembski writes, "Within a physicalist ontology intelligent agency is ultimately reducible to event-causation, as a practical matter we cannot dispense with the twin categories of conceptual and physical information" (Dembski, *No Free Lunch*, 140).

54. Dembski, *Being as Communion*, 80.

the coin for the smashed cup. Likewise, on materialist principles, it is groundless to blame a person for moral or any other failure, [because] our minds are limited to the material constitution of our brains (minds transcending brains are simply not an option for materialism), and our brains are simply more complicated arrangements of balls going down inclined planes and coins being tossed. Thus we are not in control, we are not free.[55]

The "free" choices of human agents, in other words, are simply expressions of physiological laws operating within human brains. There is no right or wrong, because impersonal forces of nature determine the outcome of every action. This materialist outlook is not only devastating for moral realists, but it also undermines Ayala's dysteleological critique against ID. To argue that God would be a "cruel" designer if he were responsible for suboptimal design implies both that cruelty exists and that suboptimal design is detectable. Neither of these implications follow if materialism is true.

Information Before Matter

Along with his critiques of naturalism and materialism, Dembski provides a plausible, albeit counterintuitive, metaphysical outlook. His proposal is that information, rather than matter, is the basic stuff of reality. Existence, he argues, is about *being in communion and exchanging information*.[56] The observable material world is thus reduced to information, rather than information reduced to matter. Dembski explains,

> [What] is real according to this information view of reality is the ability of a thing to produce a characteristic set of patterns. In other words, to say that an entity exists, and is therefore real, is to ascribe to it the ability to produce certain types of information to the exclusion of others. In Aristotelian terms, we might say that reality is gauged in terms of *potential* to produce information.[57]

This proposal might seem strange given the prevailing wisdom of materialism, but it is not unique to Dembski. Intelligent Design critic John Haught proposes a similar metaphysic when he writes, "I want to ask whether the universe itself could be thought of theologically as something

---

55. Dembski, *Being as Communion*, 11–12.
56. Dembski, *Being as Communion*, xiii.
57. Dembski, *Being as Communion*, 86.

like an information system through which a 'message' of ultimate importance is being communicated."[58] Paul Davies, likewise, argues for an information-first view of reality, defending "a view in which *information is regarded as the primary entity from which physical reality is built.*"[59] Keith Ward further suggests that information is an ultimate principle for the universe, which is "logically prior to and ontologically different from any actual physical state."[60] Thus an information-first view of reality, while still a minority position, is increasingly being explored by philosophers, physicists, theologians, and mathematicians.

In addition to the current trends related to the metaphysics of information, Dembski notes that the spirit of his metaphysical insights has a long intellectual tradition. He writes,

> In the late eighteenth and early nineteenth centuries, idealism was ascendant, identifying mind rather than matter as the fundamental reality. Both materialism and idealism are monistic, locating all of reality in a single principle, matter in the one case, mind in the other. But dualistic options also exist, such as Christian theism, which distinguishes between a nonmaterial God on the one hand and a created order on the other (a created order that includes but is not limited to matter).[61]

The materialism, idealism, and dualism of the eighteenth and nineteenth centuries can all trace their roots back to early Greek philosophy. Before Socrates, Greek philosophers introduced various metaphysical proposals for understanding the fundamental nature of reality. Thales, Anaximander, and Anaximenes, for example, each argued that ultimate reality could be reduced to one basic substance—whether water, air, or some indeterminate boundlessness. These early Milesian philosophers are often called material monists. Atomists, on the other hand, were materialists who rejected monism. They proposed that reality consisted of an infinite number of material bits. The Pythagoreans, moreover, rejected the materialist tradition and instead maintained that reality is reduced to numbers. Their mathematical conception of realty, as well as Heraclitus's notion of a fiery λόγος (*logos:* meaning word, logic, or reason), Anaxagoras's proposal that

---

58. Haught, "Information, Theology, and the Universe," 385.
59. Davies, "Universe from Bit," 95.
60. Ward, "God as the Ultimate Informational Principle," 379.
61. Dembski, *Being as Communion*, 6.

reality is governed by a universal mind, and Plato's theory of Forms, all represent potential precursors to Dembski's view.

Dembski's metaphysical project, then, builds upon a long-standing debate between materialist and non-materialist philosophers. He claims that his project is fairly broad, and therefore aspires to find common cause with contemporary non-materialists—such as Thomas Nagel, a professed atheist.[62] The purpose of finding common cause, according to Dembski, "is not because it is politically expedient in the controversy with Darwinian materialism but because theistic and naturalistic non-materialists are both attempting, without the blinders of materialism, to understand how teleology operates in nature."[63] Thus Dembski views his project as simply one non-materialist alternative to materialism.

This broad information-theoretic project, however, can funnel into a position that is uniquely and persuasively aligned with general theism. In *Being as Communion*, Dembski emphasizes that he is not contending for the primacy of information. He instead argues that information is dependent upon a fundamental intelligence. Intelligence, therefore, is prime reality according to Dembski. He explains,

> I'm not arguing for the all-sufficiency of information as such because, in my view, information is, in the end, always the product of a creative intelligence. This would make intelligence rather than information the most basic metaphysical entity, placing all-sufficiency with intelligence rather than information. Indeed, as a theist, I regard an intelligent being, God, as the prime reality. The issue here, however, is not the primacy of intelligence or teleology for metaphysics. The issue, rather, is the primacy of information for science. I am arguing that information should properly be regarded as the prime entity and object of study in science, displacing matter from its current position of eminence.[64]

62. One might also refer to other metaphysical perspectives, such as pantheism or panentheism. Pantheism is simply a spiritual form of naturalism, so Dembski's critiques of naturalism would apply to pantheism. As for panentheism, Dembski argues that panentheism is not consistent with Christian theism, and it still faces many of the problems of naturalism. According to a panentheistic conception of God, God is dependent upon matter for his existence. On this view, mind (the mind of God) is reduced to matter. According to Christian theism, however, God is the cause of matter. It does seem, therefore, that materialist monism, idealist monism, and theistic dualism are the three most viable metaphysical options. For more discussion on this topic, see Dembski, *Design Revolution*, 175–76.

63. Dembski, *Being as Communion*, 65–66.

64. Dembski, *Being as Communion*, 91. Elsewhere, Dembski explains, "From the

Dembski's distinction between intelligence and information is significant for understanding several issues related to ID, and it is especially significant for understanding the ethical issues related to the problem of dysteleology. Specifically, Dembski argues that an information-theoretic account of reality is able to ground scientific investigation. I do not have time to develop his arguments here; instead, I want to argue that a similar case can be made regarding the grounding of ethical investigation. That is, to argue that information is primary for scientific investigation is analogous to arguing that information is primary for ethical investigation. If ethicists, in other words, hope to obtain knowledge within their discipline, then they must develop a conception of reality that makes it possible to obtain moral knowledge. Dembski's information-theoretic account of reality provides justification for such hope, whereas materialism and naturalism do not.

My two goals in this chapter were (1) to demonstrate that Dembski's critiques of naturalism and materialism provide formidable reasons to reject both naturalism and materialism and (2) to introduce Dembski's information-theoretic account of reality as an alternative to naturalism and materialism. I have argued, with Dembski, that both naturalism and materialism are self-defeating, and therefore both undermine our ability to ground moral knowledge. Dembski's alternative conception of reality, on the other hand, is able to ground moral knowledge, and thus it provides a more comprehensible worldview to ground my central argument, namely, that a teleological conception of nature is necessary to make any evolutionary theodicy logically coherent.

---

vantage of materialism, matter invariably swallows up intelligence, reducing it to the motions and modifications of matter. On the other hand, from the vantage of even the most generic theism (and I include here deism, process theism, panentheism, and pantheism in addition to ethical monotheism), intelligence becomes a fundamental and irreducible feature of reality that has a say in everything. As a consequence, intelligence becomes interwoven throughout the fabric of reality, making it impossible to sever chance from intelligence or rule out that chance is the byproduct of intelligence. So the logic of one's ultimate metaphysics pushes toward one view or the other, toward chance as devoid of intelligence or toward chance as an expression, albeit indirect, of intelligence. Thus, I would say, the generic theist may regard chance as, in every case, a byproduct of intelligence" (Dembski, *Being as Communion*, 137).

6

Making Darwin a Gift to Science and Religion

IN THE PREVIOUS TWO chapters, I articulated Dembski's method for detecting design, examined his critiques of materialism and naturalism, and briefly explained his information-theoretic account of reality. Those chapters provide the groundwork for developing my central argument in this chapter, namely, that a teleological conception of nature is necessary to make any evolutionary theodicy logically coherent. By developing this argument, I am agreeing with Ayala that the mutation-selection mechanisms of evolution are useful for explaining instances of suboptimal design in biology. On the other hand, I am also disagreeing with his central thesis, which states that Darwin became a gift for theologians *by removing teleology* from biology. My thesis challenges Ayala's perspective—stating that if Darwin is considered a gift to religion, it will be because he added a more robust understanding of natural processes, and not because he subtracted design as a relevant mode of explanation in nature.

My argument in this chapter follows in two basic steps. First, I reassess Ayala's proposal that Darwin is a gift to theodicy in light of Dembski's ID project. I conclude that while Ayala's theodicy is useful, it can also be embraced by ID advocates. This first step represents a modest critique of Ayala's theological argument against ID. Second, I argue further that Ayala's evolutionary theodicy is intelligible if and only if he presupposes something similar to Dembski's information-theoretic conception of reality, which Dembski describes in the following paragraph.

> To exist is to be in communion, and to be in communion is to exchange information. Accordingly, the fundamental science, indeed the science that needs to ground all other sciences, is a theory

of communication, and not, as is widely supposed, an atomistic, reductionistic, and mechanistic science of particles or other mindless entities, which then need to be built up to ever greater orders of complexity by equally mindless principles of association, known as natural laws or algorithms or emergent properties or principles of self-organization. Within such a theory of communication, the proper object of study is not particles, but the information that passes between entities—entities in turn defined by their ability to communicate information. Accordingly, the metaphysical picture that I'm painting attempts to make good on the promise of John Wheeler, Paul Davies, and others that information is poised to replace matter "as the primary 'stuff' of the world" and that in information we have "finally arrived at the 'right' metaphor that will unify" the sciences.[1]

This second step is more ambitious as I try to demonstrate that Dembski is correct in his portrayal of reality, and that his metaphysical outlook is as much a gift to Ayala's evolutionary theodicy as Darwin is a gift to theodicy in general. If my second step fails to demonstrate this conclusion, however, it will still follow that Ayala's theological critique of ID fails.

The Value of Evolutionary Theodicies

The most fruitful aspect of Ayala's evolutionary theodicy is the claim that natural selection working on random mutations provides an adequate explanation for design in biology—including suboptimal design. This claim emphasizes the role of chance and necessity as the sole cause of suboptimal design. While I do not fully agree with Ayala's argument, I do think he points us in the right direction regarding suboptimal design. The mutation-selection processes of evolution do provide theologians with relevant mechanisms for explaining the ostensible dysfunctions and imperfections of the natural world. That is, Ayala's argument removes the requirement for theologians to explain suboptimal design in teleological terms.[2]

---

1. Dembski, *Being as Communion*, xii–xiv.

2. Of course, this proposal is not entirely novel. Paley certainly recognized that design is not the only mode of causation, which is demonstrated in his claim that chance explains wens, warts, moles, and pimples (Paley, *Natural Theology*, 38). Darwin's theory of natural selection simply demonstrates how more complex features may also arise through natural processes.

This is not to say, however, that Ayala's solution provides a defeater for ID. As seen in previous chapters, neither Dembski nor any other ID advocate rejects chance or necessity as appropriate modes of explanation in biology. The central issue is whether natural causes are supplemented by design.[3] ID advocates have never argued that every aspect of nature is designed. They also do not argue that nature exhibits optimal design. Intelligent Design argues instead that some features of nature are intentionally, whether optimally or suboptimally, designed, and teleological explanations are therefore appropriate modes of explanation in science. Dembski clarifies,

> Many biologists claim that biological systems are not actually designed and thus attempt to assimilate all biological design to either apparent or optimal design (Stephen Jay Gould, Richard Dawkins, and Francisco Ayala are masters of this strategy). This is an evasive strategy because it avoids the central question that needs to be answered, namely, the question of actual design. The automobiles that roll off the assembly lines in Detroit are intelligently designed in the sense that actual human intelligences are responsible for them. Nevertheless, even if we think Detroit manufactures the best cars in the world, it would still be wrong to say that they are optimally designed. Nor is it correct to say that they are only apparently designed.[4]

Dembski's clarification leaves ID advocates with two possible explanations for suboptimal design. First, an ID advocate may simply argue that some examples of actual design are suboptimally designed. This would not diminish the reality of actual design, since every human artifact is, in some

---

3. Dembski, *Design Revolution*, 75.

4. Dembski, "What Intelligent Design is Not," 8. In *No Free Lunch*, Dembski explains this point in the introduction: "A possible terminological confusion over the phrase 'intelligent design' needs to be cleared up. The confusion centers on what the adjective 'intelligent' is doing in the phrase 'intelligent design.' 'Intelligent' can mean nothing more than being the result of an intelligent agent, even one who acts stupidly. On the other hand, it can mean that an intelligent agent acted with consummate skill and mastery. Critics of intelligent design often understand the 'intelligent' in intelligent design in the latter sense and thus presume that intelligent design must entail optimal design. The intelligent design community, on the other hand, understands the 'intelligent' in intelligent design simply to refer to intelligent agency (irrespective of skill, mastery, or cleverness) and thus separates intelligent design from optimality of design" (Dembski, *No Free Lunch*, xvi–xvii).

sense, suboptimal. The mere presence of suboptimal design, then, does not remove the reality of actual design. Dembski further explains,

> No real designer attempts optimality in the sense of attaining perfect design. Indeed, there is no such thing as perfect design. Real designers strive for *constrained optimization*, which is something altogether different.... Design by intelligent agency [furthermore] does not preclude evil. A torture chamber replete with implements of torture is designed, and the evil of its designer does nothing to undercut the torture chamber's design.[5]

Whether one agrees or disagrees with Dembski's claim that there is no such thing as perfect design, he is correct to note that design by an intelligent agency does not preclude suboptimal design.

A second explanation for suboptimal design is to simply endorse Ayala's theodicy, namely, that imperfect design is the result of natural selection working on random mutations. Given this solution, theologians have no need to explain, for example, why God would place ganglion and bipolar cells in front of the photoreceptors in the retina.[6] Perhaps chance and necessity really do explain some features of the human eye. Dembski thus argues that a "design theorist is not committed to every biological structure being designed."[7] He explains,

> Intelligent design is not a theory about the frequency or locality or modality by which a designing intelligence intervenes in the material world. It is not an interventionist theory at all. Indeed, intelligent design is perfectly compatible with all the design in the world coming to expression by the ordinary means of secondary causes over the course of natural history, much as a computer program's

---

5. Dembski, "What Intelligent Design is Not," 8. He further writes, "Just because we can always imagine some improvement in design doesn't mean that the structure in question wasn't designed, or that the improvement can be effected, or that the improvement, even if it could be effected, would not entail deficits elsewhere. And, of course, the charge of poor design may simply be mistaken. The success of the suboptimality objection comes not from science at all, but from shifting the terms of the discussion from science to theology. In place of *How specifically can an existing structure be improved?* the question instead becomes *What sort of deity would create a structure like that?*" (Dembski, "What Intelligent Design is Not," 9).

6. This is not to say that God did not design the retina this way, only that theologians are not required to defend this claim. As far as I can tell, a Christian theologian could reasonably argue that God designed every aspect of the human eye, or he could argue that the eye developed through the interplay of chance, necessity, and design.

7. Dembski, "What Intelligent Design is Not," 10.

output comes to expression simply by running the program (and thus without monkeying with the program's operation). In fact, one way to think of the secondary causes responsible for biological evolution is as intelligently designed programs whose computational environment is the universe and whose operating system is the laws of physics and chemistry.[8]

Non-interventionist theories of evolution, therefore, are perfectly consistent with ID, provided that actual design is never negated. Dembski even argues that such positions are compatible with Christian theism when he writes,

> Christian theism is compatible with God delegating to nature many of its powers (cf. the medieval distinction between primary and secondary causes, secondary causes operating under their own power, instituted by the primary cause, God). In fact, it's not clear that Christianity requires direct divine intervention in anything except for what pertains to the salvation of humanity (e.g., the Incarnation, Resurrection, sacraments, saving faith). All of natural history, insofar as it can be distinguished from salvation history, may thus result from natural powers implanted by God but which are free from direct divine control. Christian thinkers are far from united on this point, some preferring a hands-on interventionist deity even in natural history, others preferring a hands-off laissez-faire deity. In any case, theism, whether Christian or otherwise, allows a great deal of latitude to the nature of nature, not imposing a priori constraints on nature but letting inquiry and evidence dictate what nature is and what causal power operates in it.[9]

Dembski's articulation and explanation of ID provides reason to doubt Ayala's dysteleological critique of ID, given that ID advocates can equally utilize Ayala's answer to suboptimal design.[10]

---

8. Dembski, "Making the Task of Theodicy," 221–22.

9. Dembski, *Being as Communion*, 65.

10. Dembski writes, "Dysteleology might present a problem if all design in nature were wicked or incompetent and continually flouted our moral and aesthetic yardsticks. But that is not the case. To be sure, there are microbes that seem designed to do a number on the mammalian nervous system and biological structures that look cobbled together by a long trial-and-error evolutionary process. But there are also biological examples of nano-engineering that surpass anything human engineers have concocted or entertain hopes of concocting. Dysteleology is primarily a theological problem. To exclude design from biology simply because not all examples of biological design live up to our expectations of what a designer should or should not have done is an evasion. The problem of design in biology is real and pervasive, and needs to be addressed head on and not

Ayala's theological critique of ID suffers from a greater problem, however. He contends that his evolutionary theodicy is grounded in a non-teleological conception of nature. In other words, he claims that Darwin's theory refutes any argument for actual design in biology, and, consequently, Darwin demonstrates that suboptimal design in biology is an illusion. Purported examples of suboptimal design are not immoral, therefore, because a personal agent did not create such examples. Only personal agents can commit immoral acts, but Darwin's great discovery presumably revealed that all aspects of biological life, including imperfections, are the result of unguided and impersonal physical processes. Ayala's solution to the problem of dysteleology, then, is simply to state that there is no problem by arguing that God is not responsible for imperfect design.

As mentioned in chapter 3, this solution only addresses surface-level problems. Christian theologians have traditionally affirmed a doctrine of creation and providence, even though there are various disagreements regarding how to articulate such doctrines. Leaving those disagreements aside, even minimalistic doctrines of creation and providence show that one must take the problem of natural evil, including the problem of suboptimal design, deeper than Ayala's surface-level solution. If God created and governs the natural world, then surely God bears some responsibility for dysteleology. Ayala's solution only pushes the problem of dysteleology back a step by arguing that God is not *directly* responsible for suboptimal design. Again, Chris Doran explains,

> Ayala suggests that Christians are home free now that the "bad" design we see in the universe can be "blamed on/attributed to" evolutionary processes rather than God. It seems to me that the question that Ayala avoids is the question that still must be asked: Who created the laws that govern evolutionary processes? If we pursue this avenue of thought, then the issue is not whether the design of the universe or particular features in our universe are bad, imperfect, or cruel, but rather whether God instilling the universe with the freedom to "create" itself through evolutionary processes is really worth it.[11]

sidestepped because our presuppositions about design happen to rule out imperfect design. Nature is a mixed bag. It is not William Paley's happy world of everything in delicate harmony and balance. It is not the widely caricatured Darwinian world of nature red in tooth and claw. Nature contains evil design, jerry-built design, and exquisite design. Science needs to come to terms with design as such and not dismiss it in the name of dysteleology" (Dembski, *No Free Lunch*, xvi).

11. Doran, "From Atheism to Theodicy," 340.

Doran highlights what I call *the hard problem of dysteleology*.¹² Why would God create a world governed by chance and necessity that eventually gives rise to suboptimal design and other cases of natural evil? Ayala's initial explanation does not address this deeper problem.

This is not to say, as already mentioned, that Ayala never attempts to address this problem. In his book *Am I a Monkey?* Ayala acknowledges this deeper problem and offers a brief response:

> Some anti-religious authors, as well as other critics, have argued that the process of evolution by natural selection does not discharge God's responsibility for the dysfunctions and cruelties of the living world because, for people of faith, God is the Creator of the universe and thus would be accountable for its consequences, direct or indirect. If God is omnipotent, the argument would say, He could have created a world where such things as cruelty, predation, and human miscarriages would not occur.¹³

Ayala then offers a potential solution:

> A world of life with evolution is much more exciting; it is a creative world where new species arise, complex ecosystems come about, and humans have evolved. This account will not satisfy some people of faith, and many unbelievers will surely find it less than cogent. But I am suggesting that it may provide the beginning of an explanation for many people of faith.¹⁴

I introduced some criticisms of Ayala's "more exciting theodicy" in chapter 3, but now I want to draw attention to a more crucial point.¹⁵ Ayala's deeper

---

12. What I am calling the hard problem of dysteleology is analogous to what David Chalmers calls the hard problem of consciousness. Chalmers argues that many theorists working on the problem of consciousness are only looking at superficial correlations between brain states and mental states, whereas the hard problem of consciousness seeks to determine why any configuration of neural firings would give rise to subjective experience. Similarly, Ayala is addressing superficial explanations for how chance and necessity might explain examples of suboptimal design. Such explanations might address the easy problem of dysteleology, but they do not address the hard problem. Even if Ayala's answers are correct, they do not explain why God would create a world, governed by chance and necessity, that eventually gives rise to suboptimal structures in biology. This later mystery is what I mean by "the hard problem of dysteleology."

13. Ayala, *Am I a Monkey?*, 78.

14. Ayala, *Am I a Monkey?*, 80.

15. For a persuasive critique of Ayala's suggestion, see Putz, "Love Actually," 345–61. Putz writes, "In Ayala's model, the subject of the creative that seems to be the focus of divine interest is the universe. It is this cosmic creativity, then, that needs to be preserved,

theodicy assumes a teleological outlook on creation, since he is implicitly proposing that God designed a world governed by unguided evolutionary processes because "a world of life with evolution is much more exciting." This theodicy is not intelligible without teleology. Dembski recognizes this point and compares Ayala's theodicy with a mugger who "brutalizes someone with his own hands" versus a mugger who "employs a vicious dog on a leash."[16] In both cases, the mugger is held responsible.

Thus, Ayala's solution to the easy problem of dysteleology is to remove teleology from biology, but his solution to the hard problem of dysteleology invokes a deeper teleological explanation, namely, that God purposed a world governed by unguided evolution because such a world is more exciting than a world without unguided evolution. At the deepest level, teleology is needed to ground Ayala's theodicy.[17]

---

even at the price of the suffering of individual life within it. But this conflicts with traditional doctrines of God according to which God has an invested interest in each and every one creature, animated or not, sentient or non-sentient" (Putz, "Love Actually," 349).

16. Dembski, *End of Christianity*, 164. Dembski writes, "In turning the table on [ID], Ayala has in fact turned it 360 degrees. The table is therefore back to where it was before, and the problem he meant to shift to [ID] confronts him still. Ayala worries that a God who creates by direct intervention must be held accountable for all the bad designs in the world. Ayala's proposed solution is therefore to have God set up a world in which evolution (by natural selection) brings about bad designs. But how does this address the underlying difficulty, which is that a creator God has set up the conditions under which bad design emerges? In the one case, God acts directly; in the other, indirectly. But a creator God, as the source of all being, is as responsible in the one case as in the other" (Dembski, *End of Christianity*, 163).

17. One could also argue that Ayala's solution to the easy problem also presupposes teleology. Dembski writes, "The line I find most convincing is that evil always 'parasitizes' good. Indeed, all our words for evil presuppose a good that has been perverted. Impurity presupposes purity, unrighteousness presupposes righteousness, deviation presupposes a way from which we've departed, sin presupposes a target that was missed.... Dysteleology, the perversion of design in nature, is real. It is evident all around us. But how do we explain it? The scientific naturalist explains dysteleology by claiming that the design in nature is only apparent, that it arose through mutation and natural selection (or some other natural mechanisms), and that imperfection, cruelty, and waste are to be fully expected from such mechanisms" (Dembski, "What Intelligent Design is Not," 10–11). If evil always "parasitizes" good, then one could also argue that suboptimal design always "parasitizes" actual design.

Teleology and Evolutionary Theodicies

When evaluating the merits of Ayala's evolutionary theodicy, therefore, one must filter his theodicy through a teleological lens. This filtering is necessary both from a theological and philosophical perspective. As for theology, many theologians respond to the problem of natural evil by factoring in eschatological considerations. If theological concepts like the hope of salvation, redemption, or new creation play any role in our understanding of predation, animal suffering, dysfunctions, and suboptimal design, then teleology is implicitly assumed in such concepts. Christopher Southgate, for example, writes,

> The evolutionary process, as Arthur Peacocke notes, "is characterized by propensities toward increase in complexity, information-processing and storage, consciousness, sensitivity to pain and even self-consciousness." It is hard ... to imagine that these longer-term propensities are not also reflections of the divine desire. To deny the existence of that divine desire to relate to organisms with more and more complex consciousness is to be unable to say that a primate's life contains greater value than its most primitive evolutionary ancestors.... The scheme I am developing here is *a strongly teleological one*. It affirms the value of every creature, both as a good of itself and as a vital component of an ecosystem.[18]

Southgate's evolutionary theodicy—which is more theologically insightful than Ayala's—explicitly acknowledges the role teleology plays when attempting to explain natural evil. Thus there is good reason to argue that teleology is necessary for theology.

As for philosophy, teleology is equally significant. Ayala's central argument is that Darwin is a gift to theodicy because he removed teleological explanations from biology. This bold proposal brings up many unanswered questions. How exactly did Darwin's contribution of natural selection distinguish teleological explanations from nonteleological explanations in biology? Is modern biology really in the business of ruling out teleological causes? Is Ayala making a scientific argument or philosophical argument when he rules out teleology?

One of the more common critiques directed at ID advocates is that they are not really pursuing scientific questions. Such a critique, however, can be raised against Ayala as well. He does not construct any scientific

---

18. Southgate, *Groaning of Creation*, 71.

argument to establish his claim that chance and necessity are the only modes of causation in the natural world. Indeed, he cannot establish such a claim using the tools of science. Questions pertaining to the ontology of chance, necessity, and design are philosophical questions about the nature of nature. Intelligent Design advocates like Dembski recognize this, and therefore they are often more astute in providing philosophical defenses for the notion of design in biology. My philosophical defense for design, therefore, is similar to other defenses that have been offered. In particular, I build upon Dembski's work to argue that Ayala needs design in order to make his solution to suboptimal design intelligible.

To develop this argument, I put forward two propositions. First, Dembski's information-theoretic conception of reality provides epistemic warrant for thinking that moral facts exist and are discoverable. Second, the concept of design provides epistemic warrant for thinking that human conscious agents are capable of discovering moral facts, whereas *chance and necessity alone* are unable to provide such a warrant. If both of these propositions are defensible, then there is good reason to conclude that any coherent evolutionary theodicy will require teleology.

To defend my first proposition, I contend that any evolutionary theodicy, including solutions to the problem of suboptimal design, require a basic commitment to moral realism. That is, one must commit to the idea that moral facts are objective and grounded in a reality outside of human perceptions and judgments. If one cannot defend this claim, then there is no basis for making moral judgments about the natural world. In other words, meaningful moral judgments about nature's design suggest that nature reveals moral information. But how could nature reveal moral information if nature is governed solely by chance and necessity? Materialists and naturalists who use the problem of natural evil as a defeater for theism must answer this question.

Dembski, on the other hand, turns the question on its head by arguing that information, as opposed to matter, is fundamental. According to this metaphysical outlook, chance, design, and necessity are all appropriate modes of explanation when examining the natural world. Dembski writes, "Information . . . tends to be conceived in material terms, as a property of matter. But what if information cannot be reduced to matter? To turn the tables even more sharply, what if matter itself is an expression of information?"[19] This counterintuitive question highlights a crucial

---

19. Dembski, *Being as Communion*, 1.

issue underlying moral realism and the problem of dysteleology. If materialism really is the correct conception of reality, then a moral fact must be conceived in material terms as a property of matter. And yet, moral facts are deeply connected to personal agency. Put differently, it is incoherent talk about moral values without referencing a moral valu*er*.[20] But what is a moral valu*er* if not a personal agent? Disconnecting moral facts from conscious judgments makes it incompressible to think about moral facts in the first place.

One can recognize this point simply by attempting to describe the concept of a moral fact. Doing this is much more difficult than, say, describing a physical fact. Physical facts are somewhat easy to define within a materialistic framework, since physical facts occupy space and possess mass. One can see physical facts. One can hold physical facts. There is nothing apparently mysterious about physical facts. Moral facts, however, do seem mysterious when conceived in material terms. One does not see moral facts nor can one hold moral facts. How then can one clearly articulate a moral fact?

This question is much less difficult to answer if something similar to Dembski's information-theoretic conception of reality is correct. Given his alternative perspective on reality, moral facts might be defined as a particular kind of information typically embodied in material objects or events. More specifically, moral information realizes moral possibilities by intentionally ruling out immoral possibilities.[21] In other words, moral facts are deliberate forms of communication or moral judgments that are, in principle, recognized by other personal agents. Moral judgments furthermore require choice, and the distinction between choice and other forms of contingency stems from the distinction between agency and non-agency. Without agency, moral judgments cannot be communicated. And without the communication of moral judgments, moral facts or information cannot exist.

Dembski's information-theoretic conception of reality thus makes it possible to discover moral information. The communicating of moral information often occurs within embodied objects or events, since matter is the medium for information.[22] Given this outlook, one can observe a natural

---

20. Kevin Delapp critiques this view because he argues that it would make moral values contingent upon human agents, thus undermining a commitment to moral realism (Delapp, *Moral Realism*, 13). He further utilizes Plato's *Euthyphro* to argue that moral facts must exist independent of personal agency.

21. Dembski defines information generally as "about realizing possibilities by ruling out others" (Dembski, *Being as Communion*, 19).

22. Dembski, *Being as Communion*, 97.

event and, in principle, make an intelligible judgment regarding the morality of that event. To offer an example, consider Quentin Smith's story about the moral clarity he experienced while observing a predation event:

> Not long ago I was sleeping in a cabin in the woods and was awoken . . . by the sound of a struggle between two animals. Cries of terror and extreme agony rent the night, intermingled with the sounds of jaws snapping bones and flesh being torn from limbs. . . . A clearer case of a horrible event in nature, a natural evil, has never been presented to me. It seemed to me self-evident that the natural law that animals must savagely kill and devour each other in order to survive was an evil natural law and that the obtaining of this law was sufficient evidence that God did not exist.[23]

Smith's perception of this event as horrible and evil event is noteworthy. What metaphysical presuppositions about reality make Smith's perception a reliable guide to the external world? Smith certainly has a moral perception, but that does not mean his perception corresponds to a moral reality. Kenneth Miller, in fact, argues that Smith's perceptions are irrelevant since nature does not contain moral facts. The brutality of life, he contends, is simply in the eye of the beholder.[24] Smith's moral perception, therefore, does not correspond to a moral reality from Miller's perspective. He explains,

> Could evolution really be so cruel as to require . . . an apology? To answer that question we have to keep two things in mind. The first is that cruelty is relative. As a New Englander, I enjoy few things more than a lobster dinner, especially at the end of a long summer day. The preparation of that meal, from the point of view of the lobster, is an act of unmitigated cruelty, perpetrated by me, the cook. The cats patrolling our barn are lovable family pets, but I assure you that their actions in keeping that barn vermin-free meet the highest standards of viciousness. Like beauty, the brutality of life is in the eye of the beholder.[25]

Miller's sentiment parallels Ayala's natural theodicy, contending that natural events are impersonal material events that cannot communicate moral information. And if Miller is correct in this assessment, then indeed, Smith's moral perceptions about predation are irrelevant.

---

23. Smith, "Atheological Argument," 159–74.
24. Miller, *Finding Darwin's God*, 246.
25. Miller, *Finding Darwin's God*, 245–46.

If something like Dembski's information-theoretic account of reality is correct, however, then Smith's intuitions about natural evil become intelligible. Not only does Smith have moral perceptions, but his perceptions may also correspond to objective moral information. Predation-events, various examples of suboptimal design, and all natural occurrences have the potential of communicating moral information. Thus, Dembski's metaphysical insights make it possible to discover moral facts within nature, whereas materialism does not.

The materialist's problem only gets worse when one reflects on the role human agents play in making moral judgments. To claim that moral facts are discoverable in principle does not entail that human agents are capable of discovering such facts. Such an entailment assumes that one's cognitive faculties are calibrated for detecting moral facts in the external world. Given materialism, this assumption is unwarranted for two reasons. First, the materialist has yet to solve the mystery of consciousness, which John Searle articulates in the following question: "How exactly do brain processes cause conscious states and how exactly are those states realized in brain structures?"[26]

Materialists have certainly attempted to answer this question, but so far their suggestions are inconclusive. Searle, for example, answers his own question by stating that consciousness is "a biological phenomenon in exactly the same sense as digestion, growth, or photosynthesis."[27] He compares the mystery of consciousness to the mystery of the liquidity of water. When one understands the concept of liquidity, one realizes that the alleged mystery is superficial. Liquidity is not an additional substance added to water; rather, it is a particular state of the H_2O molecules. Likewise, consciousness is not an additional substance added to brain function. Consciousness is simply a particular state of neurological firings in the brain. To distinguish mental states from brain states, then, is to explain the same event, only at a different level of explanation. Searle writes,

26. Searle, "Consciousness," 727.

27. Searle, "Consciousness," 727. Searle defines consciousness as consisting of "inner, qualitative, subjective states and processes of sentience or awareness. Consciousness, so defined, begins when we wake in the morning from a dreamless sleep and continues until we fall asleep again, die, go into a coma, or otherwise become "unconscious." It includes all of the enormous variety of the awareness that we think of as characteristic of our waking life. It includes everything from feeling a pain, to perceiving objects visually, to states of anxiety and depression, to working out crossword puzzles, playing chess, trying to remember your aunt's phone number, arguing about politics, or to just wishing you were somewhere else" (Searle, "Consciousness," 727–28).

> "The problem of consciousness" is the problem of explaining exactly how neurobiological processes in the brain *cause* our subjective states of awareness or sentience; how exactly these states are *realized in* the brain structures; and how exactly consciousness *functions* in the overall economy of the brain and therefore how it functions in our lives generally. If we could answer the causal questions—what causes consciousness and what does it cause—I believe the answers to the other questions would be relatively easy. That is, if we knew the whole causal story then such questions as "Where exactly are such and such conscious processes located in the brain, and why do we need them?" would fall into place. So stated, the problem of consciousness is a scientific research project like any other.[28]

He continues,

> The mystery of consciousness will gradually be removed when we solve the biological problem of consciousness. The mystery is not a metaphysical obstacle to ever understanding how the brain works; rather the sense of mystery derives from the fact that at present we not only do not know how it works, but we do not even have a clear idea of how the brain *could* work to cause consciousness. We do not understand how such a thing is even possible. But we have been in similar situations before. A hundred years ago it seemed a mystery that mere matter could be *alive*. And debates raged between mechanists who sought a mechanical, chemical explanation of life and vitalists who thought any such explanation was impossible, who thought that any explanation required us to postulate a "vital force," an "elan vital" that stood outside of mere chemical processes and made life possible. Today it is hard for us even to recover the sense of difficulty our great-grandparents' generation experienced over this issue. The mystery was resolved not just because the mechanists won and the vitalists lost the debate, but because we got a much richer conception of the mechanism involved. Similarly with the brain. The sense of mystery will be removed when we understand the biology of consciousness with the same depth of understanding that we now understand the biology of life.[29]

Searle's approach to the problem of consciousness, therefore, is to propose that consciousness will be understood when cognitive scientists find the

---

28. Searle, *Mystery of Consciousness*, 192–93.
29. Searle, *Mystery of Consciousness*, 201.

precise correlations between neurobiological processes in the brain and our subjective states. Once those correlations are made, the problem of consciousness is solved. Searle admits cognitive scientists are not even close to completing this project, but he is confident that the work will be accomplished in time.

David Chalmers, on the other hand, is not confident that biology will reveal a straightforward solution. He argues that Searle's project only advances the easy problem of consciousness. The easy problem of consciousness can be solved, in principle, by developing computational models that explain the precise relationships between neural mechanisms and particular functions.[30] Chalmers refers to this project as the search for neural correlates of consciousness (NCC). He explains,

> A neural correlate of consciousness can be characterized as a minimal neural system that is directly associated with states of consciousness. Presumably the brain as a whole is a neural system associated with states of consciousness, but not every part of the brain is associated equally with consciousness. The NCC project aims to isolate relatively limited parts of the brain (or relatively specific features of neural processing) that correlate directly with subjective experience.[31]

Chalmers agrees that the NCC project is useful, but it cannot address the central question confronting those working on the hard problem of consciousness, namely, why is the performance of certain brain functions accompanied by subjective experience?[32] Put differently, why would a particular configuration of neural activity give rise to a first-person perspective? Or how does one move from ontological objectivity to ontological subjectivity? Even if neurobiologists eventually map every brain state/mental state correlation, Chalmers argues that they will not arrive any closer to answering the hard problem of consciousness.

Chalmers thus maintains that those working on the problem of consciousness need to address the problem from a different perspective. Specifically, he argues that one needs to reject traditional materialism and then introduce radically new ways of thinking about the fundamental aspects of reality:[33]

30. Chalmers, *Character of Consciousness*, 7.
31. Chalmers, *Character of Consciousness*, 44.
32. Chalmers, *Character of Consciousness*, 8.
33. Thomas Nagel argues that this hard problem of consciousness is a problem

> I suggest that a theory of consciousness should take experience as fundamental. We know that a theory of consciousness requires the addition of *something* fundamental to our ontology, as everything in physical theory is compatible with the absence of consciousness.... We will take experience itself as a fundamental feature of the world, alongside mass, charge, and space-time. If we take experience as fundamental, then we can go about the business of constructing a theory of experience.... This position qualifies as a variety of dualism as it postulates basic properties over and above the properties invoked by physics. But it is an innocent version of dualism, entirely compatible with the scientific view of the world. Nothing in this approach contradicts anything in physical theory; we simply need to add further *bridging* principles to explain how experience arises from physical processes. There is nothing particularly spiritual or mystical about this theory—its overall shape is like that of a physical theory, with a few fundamental entities connected by fundamental laws. It expands the ontology slightly, to be sure, but Maxwell did the same thing. Indeed, the overall structure of this position is entirely naturalistic, allowing both that the universe ultimately comes down to a network of basic entities obeying simple laws and that there eventually may be a theory of consciousness cast in terms of such laws. If the position is to have a name, *naturalistic dualism* is a good choice.[34]

Chalmers's suggestion that consciousness is a fundamental feature of the world alongside mass, charge, and space-time, is a type of explanation that would be consistent with what I am suggesting in this chapter. I agree with Chalmers that conscious experience is best understood as a fundamental feature of the world, and is therefore not reducible to something more fundamental.[35] I disagree with Chalmers, however, that consciousness exists

---

specifically when one presumes naturalism or materialism. He explains, "Consciousness is the most conspicuous obstacle to a comprehensive naturalism that relies only on the resources of physical science. The existence of consciousness seems to imply that the physical description of the universe, in spite of its richness and explanatory power, is only part of the truth, and that the natural order is far less austere than it would be if physics and chemistry accounted for everything. If we take this problem seriously, and follow its implications, it threatens to unravel the entire naturalistic world picture" (Nagel, *Mind & Cosmos*, 35).

34. Chalmers, *Character of Consciousness*, 17–18.

35. ID advocates argue that design is a fundamental feature of the world, and is therefore not reducible to chance and necessity. As a naturalist, however, Chalmers's explanation is the best explanation I have heard from a naturalistic perspective. Other naturalists working on this problem, such as Daniel Dennett, take a different approach

alongside mass, charge, and space-time. As a Christian theist, I propose that consciousness is more fundamental than mass, charge, and space-time, and that human beings are created in the image of God—thus making human consciousness analogous to God's consciousness.[36]

I mention this hard problem of consciousness because it connects to the challenges one faces when attempting to ground moral reasoning. Consciousness is fundamental for making conscious judgments, and conscious judgments are fundamental for moral reasoning. If one cannot provide a workable solution to the hard problem of consciousness, therefore, one cannot ground moral reasoning.

In addition to providing a warrant for one's moral reasoning, one must also establish a correspondence between one's moral reasoning and moral facts. Such correspondence has not been established from a materialist perspective, and it likely cannot be established in principle. This is because chance and necessity—the only modes of causation within a materialist worldview—do not have the epistemic resources needed to justify the claim that objective moral information corresponds to our conscious moral judgments. As mentioned in chapter 5, apologists and philosophers have frequently demonstrated that naturalism and materialism are self-defeating

---

than Chalmers. Dennett also recognizes the problem, but he concludes that consciousness is merely an illusion (given naturalistic presuppositions). More specifically, Dennett rejects property dualism and argues that conscious states are not real. Chalmers rejects Dennett's suggestion, arguing that the datum of consciousness is too obvious to reject. He nevertheless argues that there are hard problems of consciousness that force us to reimagine our fundamental paradigms governing our current explanations of consciousness. He reasons that if a fundamental commitment to materialism has rendered it implausible to explain consciousness, then maybe it would be better to assume that consciousness is a fundamental aspect of reality. This is panpsychism, the idea that every aspect of reality has a certain degree of consciousness. Chalmers admits his view is a bit radical, since it forces us to conclude that objects like thermostats are conscious, but he also maintains his proposal is no more radical than Dennett's proposal that consciousness is merely an illusion.

36. I specify human consciousness here because of the debate over animal consciousness. Chalmers's panpsychism would suggest that primitive forms of consciousness exist universally. Thus, all animals would have a degree of consciousness. Searle contends that humans and "higher animals are obviously conscious, but we do not know how far down the phylogenetic scale consciousness extends." He then asks, "Are fleas conscious, for example?" (Searle, *Mystery of Consciousness*, 5). Searle does not provide an answer to this question, claiming that it is not useful to worry about such inquiries. Given the argument I am making in this chapter, the question of animal consciousness is irrelevant to the strength or weakness of my case.

and lead to the problem of epistemic absurdity. In *Warrant and Proper Function*, Alvin Plantinga provides a possible solution to this problem:

> According to our notion of warrant, a belief *B* has warrant for you if and only if (1) the cognitive faculties involved in the production of *B* are functioning properly (and this is to include the relevant defeater systems as well as those systems, if any, that provide *propositional* inputs to the system in question); (2) your cognitive environment is sufficiently similar to the one for which your cognitive faculties are designed; (3) the triple of the design plan governing the production of the belief in question involves, as purpose or function, the production of true beliefs (and the same goes for elements of the design plan governing the production of input beliefs to the system in question); and (4) the design plan is a good one: that is, there is a high statistical or objective probability that a belief produced in accordance with the relevant segment of the design plan in that sort of environment is true.[37]

Plantinga's solution is noteworthy, because it suggests that design is a necessary condition for concluding that one's cognitive faculties correspond to one's cognitive environment. If Plantinga is correct, then his solution also applies to moral epistemology. To have moral knowledge about the natural world, one must assume that natural world communicates moral information. One must further assume that human judgments are produced by conscious moral agents. And last, one must assume that human judgments correspond to moral information that is instantiated in the natural world. These three assumptions are consistent with Dembski's information-theoretic account of reality, as well as Plantinga's design notion of warrant. Thus, a teleological worldview provides a basis for thinking that moral realism is true, which means that it also provides a foundation for developing a logically consistent evolutionary theodicy.

Embracing a Teleological Worldview

Of course, one might object to my argument by claiming that it is directed only at naturalists or materialists. Ayala is a theist. My response to this objection, as already mentioned, is that Ayala's evolutionary theodicy assumes a nonteleological perspective on nature, as well as a nonteleological

---

37. Plantinga, *Warrant and Proper Function*, 194.

account of human consciousness. This is perhaps most evident in the following paragraphs:

> In an important sense, the most distinctive human features are those expressed in the brain, those that account for the human mind and for human identity.... Humans (and humans alone, at least to any significant degree) have developed the capacity to adapt to hostile environments by modifying the environments according to the needs of their genes. The discovery of fire and the fabrication of clothing and shelter have allowed humans to spread from the warm tropical and subtropical regions of the Old World, to which we are biologically adapted, to the whole earth except for the frozen wastes of Antarctica. It was not necessary for wandering humans to wait until genes providing anatomical protection against cold temperatures by means of fur or hair would evolve. Nor are we humans biding our time in expectation of wings or gills; we have conquered the air and seas with artfully designed contrivances—airplanes and ships. It is the human brain (or rather, the human mind) that has made humankind the most successful living species by most meaningful standards.[38]

Ayala continues,

> One exciting biological discipline that has made great strides within the past two decades is neurobiology.... Much has been learned about how light, sound, temperature, resistance, and chemical impressions received in our sense organs trigger the release of chemical transmitters and electric potential differences that carry the signals through the nerves to the brain and elsewhere in the body.... But despite all [the] progress, neurobiology remains an infant discipline, at a stage of theoretical development comparable perhaps to that of genetics at the beginning of the twentieth century when Mendel's laws of heredity were rediscovered. Those things that count most remain shrouded in mystery: how physical phenomena become mental experiences (the feelings and sensations, called "qualia" by philosophers, that contribute the elements of consciousness) and how out of the diversity of these experiences emerges the mind, a reality with unitary properties such as free will and the awareness of self that persist throughout an individual's life. I do not believe that the mysteries of the mind are unfathomable; rather, they are puzzles that humans can solve with the methods of science and illuminate with philosophical analysis

---

38. Ayala, *Am I a Monkey?*, 10.

and reflection. And I will place my bets that, over the next half-century or so, many of these puzzles will be solved.[39]

On the surface, Ayala's statements about human consciousness are unproblematic. But when considered in the context of his other writings, he clearly maintains that consciousness developed through an unguided process of biological evolution. That is, chance and necessity is sufficient to explain the origin of human conscious agents. Again, Ayala:

> The theory of evolution manifests chance and necessity jointly intertwined in the stuff of life; randomness and determinism interlocked in a natural process that has brought forth the most complex, diverse, and beautiful entities in the universe: the organisms that populate the earth, including humans who think and love, endowed with free will and creative powers, and able to analyze the process of evolution itself that brought them into existence. This was Darwin's fundamental discovery, that there is a natural process that is creative, though not conscious.[40]

Note how Ayala includes "humans who think and love" when expressing his story of unconscious biological evolution. Thinking and loving, of course, are properties of human consciousness. It follows that human consciousness could not have been designed, since chance and necessity are the only modes of causation that exist in Ayala's conception of evolution.[41] And yet, human conscious agents are presumably able to produce artifacts through a teleological process.[42]

---

39. Ayala, *Am I a Monkey?*, 11–12.

40. Ayala, "Chance and Necessity," 238.

41. Dembski and Ayala mean different things by the word *teleology*. Ayala explains teleology as follows: "Automobiles exist and have particular configurations because they serve for transportation, and thus can be explained teleologically. Not all features of a car contribute to the purpose of efficient transportation—some features are added for aesthetic or other reason. But as long as a feature is added because it exhibits certain properties—like appeal to the aesthetic preferences of potential customer—it may be explained teleologically. Nevertheless, there may be features in a car, a knife, or any other human-made object that need not be explained teleologically. That knives have handles is to be explained teleologically, but the fact that a particular handle is made of pine rather than oak might simply be due to the availability of material. Similarly, not all features of organisms have teleological explanations" (Ayala, *Chance and Necessity*, 241).

42. Ayala writes, "Inanimate objects and processes (other than those created by humans) are not teleological because they are not directed toward specific ends, they do not exist to serve certain purposes" (Ayala, *Chance and Necessity*, 240).

This is where Ayala's worldview seems inconsistent. Human beings, he acknowledges, are products of the natural world. And if the natural causes of chance and necessity are fundamental to nature, then surely human intelligence would be reduced to chance and necessity as well. This implies, so it would seem, that any artifact created by human intelligence is likewise reduced to chance and necessity. Ayala may want to reject this reductionist way of reasoning, but his nonteleological outlook on nature cannot justify his rejection. His worldview, in other words, suffers from the same self-defeating consequences as faced by naturalism and materialism. Thus, Ayala would do well to abandon his nonteleological approach to biology.

After analyzing Ayala's evolutionary theodicy in light of Dembski's ID project, I conclude that there are fundamental problems with Ayala's nonteleological worldview. He wants to argue that both natural evil and suboptimal design undermine the ID project, and yet his worldview cannot provide a rational foundation for any of his arguments. Of course, recognizing this does not remove the problem of suboptimal design biology. Instead, it merely shows that suboptimal design cannot be addressed until teleology is first assumed. If philosophers and theologians hope to develop a coherent evolutionary theodicy, therefore, they must appreciate the insights offered by ID advocates like Dembski. Only then can Darwin become a gift to science and religion.

Bibliography

Alexander, Denis R. "Darwin's Gift to Science and Religion." *Science And Christian Belief* 20.2 (2008) 208–11.
Arnhart, Larry, Michael J. Behe, and William A. Dembski. "Conservatives, Darwin & Design: An Exchange." *First Things* 107 (2000) 23–31.
Axe, Douglas. *Undeniable: How Biology Confirms our Intuition that Life is Designed*. New York: HarperCollins, 2016.
Ayala, Francisco J. *Am I a Monkey? Six Big Questions about Evolution*. Baltimore, MD: Johns Hopkins University Press, 2010.
———. "The Baldwin Effect." In *Back to Darwin: A Richer Account of Evolution*, edited by John Cobb Jr., 193–95. Grand Rapids: Eerdmans, 2008.
———. *The Big Questions: Evolution*. London: Quercus, 2012.
———. "Biology Precedes, Culture Transcends: An Evolutionist's View of Human Nature." *Zygon* 33.4 (1998) 507–23.
———. "Chance and Necessity: Adaptation and Novelty in Evolution." In *Evolving Dialogue*, edited by J. B. Miller, 231–61. Harrisburg, PA: Trinity, 2001.
———. "Charles Darwin: Friend or Foe?" *Word & World* 29.1 (2009) 19–29.
———. *Darwin and Intelligent Design*. Minneapolis: Fortress, 2006.
———. "Darwin and Intelligent Design." In *The Blackwell Companion to Science and Christianity*, edited by J. B. Stump and Alan Padgett, 283–94. Malden, MA: Blackwell, 2012.
———. "Darwin and Intelligent Design." In *Science and Religion in Dialogue*, edited by Melville Steward, 751–66. Vol. 2. Malden, MA: Blackwell, 2010.
———. "Darwin and the Teleology of Nature." In *Science and Religion: In Search of Cosmic Purpose*, edited by John Haught, 18–41. Washington, DC: Georgetown University Press, 2000.
———. *Darwin's Gift to Science and Religion*. Washington, DC: Joseph Henry, 2007.
———. "Design without Designer: Darwin's Greatest Discovery." In *Debating Design: From Darwin to DNA*, edited by William Dembski and Michael Ruse, 55–80. Cambridge: Cambridge University Press, 2004.
———. "Egg-to-Adult, Brain-to-Mind, and Ape-to-Human Transformations." In *Back to Darwin: A Richer Account of Evolution*, edited by John Cobb Jr., 88–98. Grand Rapids: Eerdmans, 2008.

———. "Evolution beyond Biology: Comments and Responses." *Theology and Science* 7.4 (2009) 379–90.

———. "The Evolution of Life: An Overview." In *God and Evolution: A Reader*, edited by Mary Cunningham, 58–67. New York: Routledge, 2007.

———. "From Paley to Darwin: Design to Natural Selection." In *Back to Darwin: A Richer Account of Evolution*, edited by John Cobb Jr., 76–87. Grand Rapids: Eerdmans, 2008.

———. "Human Evolution: The Three Grand Challenges of Human Biology." In *The Cambridge Companion to the Philosophy of Biology*, edited by David Hull and Michael Ruse, 233–54. Cambridge: Cambridge University Press, 2007.

———. "Human Nature: One Evolutionist's View." In *Whatever Happened to the Soul?*, edited by Warren S. Brown, Nancey Murphy and H. Newton Malony, 31–48. Minneapolis: Fortress, 1998.

———. "Molecular Evolution." In *Evolution: The First Four Billion Years*, edited by Michael Ruse and Joseph Travis, 132–51. Cambridge, MA: Harvard University Press, 2009.

———. "Note on Evolution and Religion in the Light of Teilhard's Divine Milieu." *Zygon* 3.4 (1968) 426–31.

———. "Parallel Evolution." In *Faith in Science: Scientists Search for Truth*, edited by W. Mark Richardson and Gordy Slack, 6–17. New York: Routledge, 2001.

———. "Punctuated Equilibrium and Species Selection." In *Back to Darwin: A Richer Account of Evolution*, edited by John Cobb Jr., 185–92. Grand Rapids: Eerdmans, 2008.

———. "So Human an Animal: Evolution and Ethics." In *Science and Theology: The New Consonance*, edited by Ted Peters, 121–36. Boulder, CO: Westview, 1998.

———. "There Is No Place for Intelligent Design in the Philosophy of Biology: Intelligent Design Is Not Science." In *Contemporary Debates in Philosophy of Biology*, edited by Francisco Ayala and Robert Arp, 364–90. Malden, MA: Blackwell, 2010.

———. "What the Biological Sciences Can and Cannot Contribute to Ethics." In *Contemporary Debates in Philosophy of Biology*, edited by Francisco Ayala and Robert Arp, 316–36. Malden, MA: Blackwell, 2010.

Ayala, Francisco J., and John C. Avise, eds. *Essential Readings in Evolutionary Biology*. Baltimore, MD: Johns Hopkins University Press, 2014.

Behe, Michael. *Darwin Devolves: The New Science About DNA That Challenges Evolution*. New York: HarperOne, 2019.

———. *Darwin's Black Box: The Biochemical Challenge to Evolution*. New York: Free Press, 1996.

———. *The Edge of Evolution: The Search for the Limits of Darwinism*. New York: Free Press, 2007.

Behe, Michael, William Dembski, and Stephen Meyer, eds. *Science and Evidence for Design in the Universe*. San Francisco: Ignatius, 2000.

Beilby, James, ed. *Naturalism Defeated? Essays on Plantinga's Evolutionary Argument against Naturalism*. Ithaca, NY: Cornell University Press, 2002.

Cela-Conde, Camilo, and Francisco J. Ayala. *Human Evolution: Trails from the Past*. Oxford: Oxford University Press, 2007.

Chalmers, David J. *The Character of Consciousness*. Oxford: Oxford University Press, 2010.

Churchland, Patricia. "Epistemology in the Age of Neuroscience." *Journal of Philosophy* 84 (1987) 544–53.

Cobb, John, Jr., ed. *Back to Darwin: A Richer Account of Evolution*. Grand Rapids: Eerdmans, 2008.

Comfort, Nathaniel C., ed. *The Panda's Black Box*. Baltimore, MD: Johns Hopkins University Press, 2007.

Copan, Paul, and William L. Craig, eds. *The Kalām Cosmological Argument: Scientific Evidence for the Beginning of the Universe*. New York: Bloomsbury, 2018.

Coyne, Jerry. "Intelligent Design: The Faith That Dare Not Speak Its Name." In *Intelligent Thought: Science Versus the Intelligent Design Movement*, edited by John Brockman, 3–23. New York: Vintage, 2006.

Craig, William L., and J. P. Moreland, eds. *The Blackwell Companion to Natural Theology*. Malden, MA: Blackwell, 2012.

Darwin, Charles. *On the Origin of Species*. Oxford: Oxford University Press, 2008.

Darwin, Francis, ed. *The Life and Letters of Charles Darwin Including an Autobiographical Chapter*. New York: D. Appleton and Company, 1897.

Davies, Paul. "Universe from Bit." In *Information and the Nature of Reality*, edited by Paul Davies and Niels H. Gregersen. 83–117. Cambridge: Cambridge University Press, 2014.

Davis, Percival, and Dean H. Kenyon. *Of Pandas and People: The Central Question of Biological Origins*. 2nd ed. Dallas, TX: Haughton, 1993.

Dawkins, Richard. *The Blind Watchmaker: Why the Evidence of Evolution Reveals a Universe without Design*. New York: W. W. Norton, 1996.

———. *Climbing Mount Improbable*. New York: W.W. Norton, 1996.

———. *The God Delusion*. New York: Houghton Mifflin, 2006.

———. *The Greatest Show on Earth: The Evidence for Evolution*. New York: Free Press, 2009.

Delapp, Kevin. *Moral Realism*. New York: Bloomsbury Academic, 2013.

Dembski, William. "Are We Spiritual Machines?" *First Things* 96 (1999) 25–31.

———. *Being as Communion: A Metaphysics of Information*. Burlington, VT: Ashgate, 2014.

———. "Can Evolutionary Algorithms Generate Specified Complexity?" In *From Complexity to Life*, edited by Niels Gregersen, 93–113. Oxford: Oxford University Press, 2003.

———. "Darwin's Devolution: Design without Designer." In *Evolutionary and Molecular Biology*, edited by Robert John Russell, et al., 101–16. Vatican City: Vatican Observatory, 1998.

———. "Dealing with the Backlash Against Intelligent Design." In *Darwin's Nemesis: Phillip Johnson and the Intelligent Design Movement*, edited by William Dembski, 81–104. Downers Grove, IL: InterVarsity, 2006.

———. "The Design Argument." In *Science & Religion: A Historical Introduction*, edited by Gary Ferngren, 335–44. Baltimore, MD: Johns Hopkins University Press, 2002.

———. *The Design Inference: Eliminating Chance through Small Probabilities*. Cambridge: Cambridge University Press, 1998.

———. *The Design of Life: Discovering Signs of Intelligence in Biological Systems*. Richardson, TX: Foundation for Thought and Ethics, 2008.

———. *The Design Revolution: Answering the Toughest Questions about Intelligent Design*. Downers Grove, IL: InterVarsity, 2004.

———. *The End of Christianity: Finding a Good God in an Evil World*. Nashville: B & H, 2009.

———. "Evil, Creation and Intelligent Design." In *God and Evil: The Case for God in a World Filled with Pain*, edited by Chad Meister and James Dew Jr., 259–69. Downers Grove, IL: InterVarsity, 2013.

———. "The Fallacy of Contextualism." In *Unapologetic Apologetics: Meeting the Challenges of Theological Studies*, edited by William Dembski and Jay Wesley Richards, 44–56. Downers Grove, IL: InterVarsity, 2001.

———. "God's Use of Chance." *Perspectives on Science and Christian Faith* 60.4 (2008) 248–50.

———. "Intelligent Design as a Theory of Information." In *Intelligent Design Creationism and Its Critics: Philosophical, Theological, and Scientific Perspectives*, edited by Robert Pennock, 553–74. Cambridge, MA: Massachusetts Institute of Technology, 2001.

———. *Intelligent Design: The Bridge between Science and Theology*. Downers Grove, IL: InterVarsity, 1999.

———. "The Logical Underpinnings of Intelligent Design." In *Debating Design: From Darwin to DNA*, edited by William Dembski and Michael Ruse, 311–30. New York: Cambridge University Press, 2004.

———. "Making the Task of Theodicy Impossible? Intelligent Design and the Problem of Evil." In *The Evolution of Evil*, edited by Gaymon Bennett, et al., 218–33. Göttingen, Germany: Vandenhoecky & Ruprecht, 2008.

———. "The Myths of Darwinism." In *Uncommon Dissent: Intellectuals Who Find Darwinism Unconvincing*, edited by William Dembski, xvii–xxxvii. Wilmington, DE: Intercollegiate Studies Institute, 2004.

———. *No Free Lunch: Why Specified Complexity Cannot Be Purchased without Intelligence*. Lanham, MD: Rowman & Littlefield, 2002.

———. "Not Even False? Reassessing the Demise of British Natural Theology." *Philosophia Christi* 1.1 (1999) 17–43

———. "On the Very Possibility of Intelligent Design." In *The Creation Hypothesis: Scientific Evidence for an Intelligent Designer*, edited by J. P. Moreland, 113–38. Downers Grove, IL: InterVarsity: 1994.

———. "The Problem of Error in Scripture." In *Unapologetic Apologetics: Meeting the Challenges of Theological Studies*, edited by William Dembski and Jay Wesley Richards, 79–94. Downers Grove, IL: InterVarsity, 2001.

———. "Reinstating Design within Science." In *Unapologetic Apologetics: Meeting the Challenges of Theological Studies*, edited by William Dembski and Jay Wesley Richards, 239–57. Downers Grove, IL: InterVarsity, 2001.

———. "Science and Design." *First Things* 86 (1998) 21–27.

———. "Signs of Intelligence: A Primer on the Discernment of Intelligent Design." In *Signs of Intelligence: Understanding Intelligent Design*, edited by William Dembski and James Kushiner, 171–92. Grand Rapids: Brazos, 2001.

———. "Specification: The Pattern that Signifies Intelligence." *Philosophia Christi* 7.2 (2005) 299–343.

———. "The Task of Apologetics." In *Unapologetic Apologetics: Meeting the Challenges of Theological Studies*, edited by William Dembski and Jay Wesley Richards, 31–43. Downers Grove, IL: InterVarsity, 2001.

———. "The Third Mode of Explanation: Detecting Evidence of Intelligent Design in the Sciences." In *Science and Evidence for Design in the Universe*, edited by Michael Behe, William Dembski, and Stephen Meyer, 17–52. San Francisco: Ignatius, 2000.

BIBLIOGRAPHY

———. "What Every Theologian Should Know about Creation, Evolution & Design." In *Unapologetic Apologetics: Meeting the Challenges of Theological Studies*, edited by William Dembski and Jay Wesley Richards, 221–38. Downers Grove, IL: InterVarsity, 2001.

———. "What Intelligent Design is Not." In *Signs of Intelligence: Understanding Intelligent Design*, edited by William Dembski and James Kushiner, 7–23. Grand Rapids: Brazos, 2001.

———. "Who's God the Magic?" In *Intelligent Design Creationism and Its Critics: Philosophical, Theological, and Scientific Perspectives*, edited by Robert Pennock, 639–44. Cambridge, MA: Massachusetts Institute of Technology Press, 2001.

Dembski, William, and James Kushiner, eds. *Signs of Intelligence: Understanding Intelligent Design*. Grand Rapids: Brazos, 2001.

Dembski, William, and Jay W. Richards, eds. *Unapologetic Apologetics: Meeting the Challenges of Theological Studies*. Downers Grove, IL: InterVarsity, 2001.

Dembski, William, and Michael Ruse, eds. *Debating Design: From Darwin to DNA*. Cambridge: Cambridge University Press, 2004.

———. "Intelligent Design: A Dialogue." In *Intelligent Design: William A. Dembski & Michael Ruse in Dialogue*, edited by Robert B. Stewart, 12–43. Minneapolis: Fortress, 2007.

Dembski, William, and Robert Marks II. "Life's Conservation Law: Why Darwinian Evolution Cannot Create Biological Information." In *The Nature of Nature: Examining the Role of Naturalism in Science*, edited by Bruce Gordon and William Dembski, 360–99. Wilmington, DE: Intercollegiate Studies Institute, 2011.

Dembski, William, and Stephen C. Meyer. "Fruitful Interchange or Polite Chitchat? The Dialogue between Science and Theology." *Zygon* 33.3 (1998) 415–30.

Dennett, Daniel. *Consciousness Explained*. Boston: Little Brown, 1991.

Denton, Michael. *Evolution: A Theory in Crisis*. Bethesda, MD: Adler & Adler, 1986.

Doran, Chris. "From Atheism to Theodicy to Intelligent Design: Responding to the Work of Francisco J. Ayala." *Theology and Science* 7.4 (2009) 337–44.

Elsberry, Wesley. "Logic and Math Turn to Smoke and Mirrors: William Dembski's 'Design Inference.'" In *Scientists Confront Intelligent Design and Creationism*, edited by Andrew Petto and Laurie Godfrey, 250–71. New York: W. W. Norton & Company, 2007.

Felsenstein, Joe. "Has Natural Selection Been Refuted? The Arguments of William Dembski." In *National Center for Science Education Reports* 27 (2007) 21–26.

Gilbert, Scott F., and the Swarthmore College of Evolution. "The Aerodynamics of Flying Carpets: Why Biologists Are Loath to 'Teach the Controversy.'" In *The Panda's Black Box*, edited by Nathaniel C. Comfort. 44–45. Baltimore, MD: Johns Hopkins University Press, 2007.

Gonzalez, Guillermo, and Jay W. Richards. *The Privileged Planet: How Our Place in the Cosmos is Designed for Discovery*. New York: Regnery, 2004.

Gordon, Bruce, and William Dembski, eds. *The Nature of Nature: Examining the Role of Naturalism in Science*. Wilmington, DE: Intercollegiate Studies Institute, 2011.

Haeckel, Ernst. *The History of Creation: Or, the Development of the Earth and Its Inhabitants by the Action of Natural Causes*. Vol. 1. 6th ed. New York: Appleton, 1914.

Hasker, William. *The Emergent Self*. Ithaca, NY: Cornell University Press, 2001.

Haught, John F. "Information, Theology, and the Universe." In *Information and the Nature of Reality*, edited by Paul Davies and Niels H. Gregersen. 382–404. Cambridge: Cambridge University Press, 2014.

Heltne, Paul G. "Am I a Monkey? Six Big Questions about Evolution." *Zygon* 46.2 (2011) 500–1.

Himma, Kenneth Einar. "The Application-Conditions for Design Inferences: Why the Design Arguments Need the Help of Other Arguments for God's Existence." *International Journal for Philosophy of Religion* 57.1 (2005) 1–33.

Hull, D. L. "God of the Galapagos." *Nature* 352 (1992) 485–86.

Inwood, Brad, and L. P. Gerson, eds. *The Epicurus Reader*. Indianapolis: Hackett, 1994.

Johnson, Phillip. *Darwin on Trial*. 3rd ed. Downers Grove, IL: InterVarsity, 2010.

———. *Reason in the Balance: The Case against Naturalism in Science, Law and Education*. Downers Grove, IL: InterVarsity, 1995.

Keas, Michael N. "Collins and Dembski Offer Their Views of Theodicy and God's Creative Plan." *Perspectives on Science and Christian Faith* 62.3 (2010) 214–17.

Kelly, Christopher. "Darwin and Intelligent Design." *Science Et Esprit* 59.1 (2007) 87–91.

Kojonen, Erkki Vesa Rope. "Tensions in Intelligent Design's Critique of Theistic Evolutionism." *Zygon* 48.2 (2013) 251–73.

Koperski, Jeffrey. "Two Bad Ways to Attack Intelligent Design and Two Good Ones." *Zygon* 43.2 (2008) 433–49.

Krauss, Lawrence. *A Universe from Nothing: Why There is Something Rather than Nothing*. New York: Simon & Schuster, 2012.

Lewis, C. S. *Miracles*. New York: HarperCollins, 2001.

Lewis, Geraint F., and Luke A. Barnes. *A Fortunate Universe: Life in a Finely Tuned Cosmos*. Cambridge: Cambridge University Press, 2016.

Marks, Robert J., II, William Dembski, and Winston Ewert. *Introduction to Evolutionary Informatics*. Hackensack, NJ: World Scientific Publishing, 2017.

McCall, Bradford. "Intelligent Design: William A. Dembski & Michael Ruse in Dialogue." *Christian Scholar's Review* 38.2 (2009) 305–7.

McMullin, Ernan. "Darwin and the Other Christian Tradition." *Zygon* 46.2 (2011) 291–316.

Meyer, Stephen. *Darwin's Doubt: The Explosive Origin of Animal Life and the Case for Intelligent Design*. New York: HarperOne, 2013.

———. *Signature in the Cell: DNA and the Evidence for Intelligent Design*. New York: HarperOne, 2009.

Miller, Kenneth R. *Finding Darwin's God: A Scientist's Search for Common Ground Between God and Evolution*. New York: HarperCollins, 1999.

Monod, Jacques. *Chance and Necessity*. New York: Vintage, 1972.

Moreland, J. P. *Scientism and Secularism: Learning to Respond to a Dangerous Ideology*. Wheaton, IL: Crossway, 2018.

Murray, Michael J. "Natural Providence: Reply to Dembski." *Faith and Philosophy* 23.3 (2006) 337–41.

Nagel, Thomas. *Mind & Cosmos: Why the Materialist Neo-Darwinian Conception of Nature is Almost Certainly False*. Oxford: Oxford University Press, 2012.

Nguyen, L., et al. "Phylogenetic Analyses of the Constituents of Type III Protein Secretion Systems." *Journal of Molecular Microbiology and Biotechnology* 2.2 (2000) 125–44.

Numbers, Ronald. *The Creationists: From Scientific Creationism to Intelligent Design*. Cambridge, MA: Harvard University Press, 2006.

Paley, William. *Natural Theology*. Oxford: Oxford University Press, 2006.

Pennock, Robert T., ed. *Intelligent Design Creationism and Its Critics: Philosophical, Theological, and Scientific Perspectives*. Cambridge, MA: Massachusetts Institute of Technology Press, 2001.

Perakh, Mark. "There Is a Free Lunch after All: Dembski's Wrong Answers to Irrelevant Questions." In *Why Intelligent Design Fails: A Scientific Critique of the New Creationism*, edited by Matt Young and Taner Edis, 153–71. New Brunswick, NJ: Rutgers University Press, 2004.

———. *Unintelligent Design*. New York: Prometheus, 2004.

Petto, Andrew, and Laurie Godfrey, eds. *Scientists Confront Intelligent Design and Creationism*. New York: Norton & Company, 2007.

Plantinga, Alvin. "The Evolutionary Argument against Naturalism: An Initial Statement of the Argument." In *Naturalism Defeated? Essays on Plantinga's Evolutionary Argument against Naturalism*, edited by James Beilby, 1–14. Ithaca, NY: Cornell University Press, 2002.

———. *Warrant and Proper Function*. Oxford: Oxford University Press, 1993.

———. *Warrant: The Current*. Oxford: Oxford University Press, 1993.

———. *Warranted Christian Belief*. Oxford: Oxford University Press, 2000.

———. *Where the Conflict Really Lies: Science, Religion & Naturalism*. Oxford: Oxford University Press, 2011.

Popper, Karl. *The Two Fundamental Problems of the Theory of Knowledge*. Edited by Troels E. Hansen. New York: Routledge, 2009.

Putz, Oliver. "Love Actually: A Theodicy Response to Suffering in Nature. In Dialogue with Francisco Ayala." *Theology and Science* 7.4 (2009) 245–361.

Ray, John. *The Wisdom of God Manifested in the Works of Creation: In Two Parts*, 1691.

Reppert, Victor. "The Argument from Reason." In *The Blackwell Companion to Natural Theology*, edited by William L. Craig and J. P. Moreland, 344–90. Malden, MA: Blackwell, 2012.

Russell, Robert John. "Is Evil Evolving?" *Dialog* 42.3 (2003) 309–15.

Scott, Eugenie C. *Evolution Vs. Creation: An Introduction*. Los Angeles: University of California Press, 2004.

Searle, John R. *The Mystery of Consciousness*. New York: NYRB, 1997.

Shermer, Michael. *Why Darwin Matters: The Case Against Intelligent Design*. New York: Henry Holt, 2006.

Smith, Quentin. "An Atheological Argument from Evil Natural Laws." *International Journal for Philosophy of Religion* 29.3 (1991) 159–74.

Southgate, Christopher. *The Groaning of Creation: God, Evolution, and the Problem of Evil*. Louisville: Westminster John Knox, 2008.

Stewart, Robert B., ed. *Intelligent Design: William A. Dembski & Michael Ruse in Dialogue*. Minneapolis: Fortress, 2007.

Ten Elshof, Gregg. "The End of Christianity: Finding a Good God in an Evil World." *Religious Studies Review* 36.3 (2010) 211.

Thaxton, Charles, Walter Bradley, and Roger Olson. *The Mystery of Life's Origin: Reassessing Current Theories*. Dallas, TX: Lewis and Stanley, 1984.

Ward, Keith. "God as the Ultimate Informational Principle." In *Information and the Nature of Reality*, edited by Paul Davies and Niels H. Gregersen, 357–81. Cambridge: Cambridge University Press, 2014.

BIBLIOGRAPHY

Woodward, Thomas. *Darwin Strikes Back: Defending the Science of Intelligent Design.* Grand Rapids: Baker, 2006.

———. *Doubts about Darwin: A History of Intelligent Design.* Grand Rapids: Baker, 2003.

Wolpert, D. H. "William Dembski's Treatment of No Free Lunch Theorems Is Written in Jell-O." *Mathematical Review* 12 (2003) 12

Young, Matt, and Taner Edis, eds. *Why Intelligent Design Fails: A Scientific Critique of the New Creationism.* New Brunswick, NJ: Rutgers University Press

www.ingramcontent.com/pod-product-compliance
Lightning Source LLC
Chambersburg PA
CBHW051940160426
43198CB00013B/2234